NOTES ON A SHIPWRECK

ALSO BY DAVIDE ENIA

On Earth as It Is in Heaven

NOTES *on a* SHIPWRECK

A Story of Refugees, Borders, and Hope

Davide Enia

Translated from the Italian by Antony Shugaar

OTHER PRESS / NEW YORK

Originally published in Italian as *Appunti per un naufragio* in 2017
by Sellerio Editore, Palermo, Italy.

English translation copyright © 2019 Antony Shugaar

Production editor: Yvonne E. Cárdenas
Text designer: Jennifer Daddio
This book was set in Horley Old Style
by Alpha Design & Composition of Pittsfield, NH

1 3 5 7 9 10 8 6 4 2

LIBRARY OF CONGRESS CATALOGING-IN-PUBLICATION DATA

Names: Enia, Davide, 1974– author. | Shugaar, Antony, translator.
Title: Notes on a shipwreck : a story of refugees, borders, and hope / Davide Enia ;
translated from the Italian by Antony Shugaar.
Other titles: Appunti per un naufragio. English
Description: New York : Other Press, 2019. | Originally published in Italian as Appunti
per un naufragio in 2017 by Sellerio editore via Enzo ed Elvira Sellerio 50 Palermo.
Identifiers: LCCN 2018029577 (print) | LCCN 2018044304 (ebook) |
ISBN 9781590519103 (ebook) | ISBN 9781590519080 (paperback)
Subjects: LCSH: Enia, Davide, 1974—Travel—Italy—Lampedusa Island. |
Enia, Davide, 1974—Family. | Authors, Italian—21st century—Biography. |
Lampedusa Island (Italy—Emigration and immigration—History—21st century. |
Shipwrecks—Mediterranean Sea—History—21st century. | BISAC: BIOGRAPHY
& AUTOBIOGRAPHY / Personal Memoirs. | SOCIAL SCIENCE / Emigration &
Immigration. | HISTORY / Modern / 21st Century.
Classification: LCC PQ4905.N53 (ebook) | LCC PQ4905.N53 Z46 2019 (print) |
DDC 853/.92—dc23
LC record available at https://lccn.loc.gov/2018029577

FOR SILVIA,

my landing place

On Lampedusa, a fisherman once asked me: "You know what fish has come back? Sea bass."

Then he'd lit a cigarette and smoked the whole thing down to the butt in silence.

"And you know why sea bass have come back to this stretch of sea? You know what they eat? That's right."

And he'd stubbed out his cigarette and turned to go.

There was nothing more, truly, to be said.

What had stuck with me about Lampedusa were the calluses on the hands of the fishermen; the stories they told of constantly finding dead bodies when they hauled in their nets ("What do you mean, 'constantly'?" and they'd say, "Do you know what 'constantly' means? Constantly"); scattered refugee boats rusting in the sunlight, perhaps nowadays the only honest form of testimony left to us—corrosion, grime, rust—of what's happening in this period of history; the islanders' doubts about the meaning of it all; the word "landing," misused for years, because by now these were all genuine rescues, with the refugee boats escorted into port and the poor devils led off to the Temporary Settlement Center; and the Lampedusans who dressed them with their own clothing in a merciful response that sought neither spotlights nor publicity, but just because it was cold out and those were bodies in need of warmth.

HAZE BLURRED our line of sight.

The horizon shimmered.

I noticed for what must have been the thousandth time how astonished I was to see how Lampedusa could unsettle its guests, creating in them an overwhelming sense of estrangement. The sky so close that it almost seemed about to collapse on top of us. The ever-present voice of the wind. The light that hits you from all directions. And before your eyes, always, the sea, the eternal crown of joy and thorns that surrounds everything. It's an island on which the elements hammer at you with nothing able to stop them. There are no shelters. You're pierced by the environment, riven by the light and the wind. No defense is possible.

It had been a long, long day.

I heard my father's voice calling my name, while the sirocco tossed and tangled my thoughts.

I HAPPENED TO MEET the scuba diver at a friend's house.

It was just the two of us.

The first, persistent sensation was this: He was huge.

His first words were these: "No tape recorders."

He went over and sat down on the other side of the table from me and crossed his arms.

He kept them folded across his chest the whole time.

"I'm not talking about October third," he added, his mouth snapping shut after these words in a way that defied argument.

His tone of voice was consistently low and measured, in sharp contrast with that imposing bulk. Sometimes, in his phrases, uttered with the sounds of his homeland—he was born in the mountains of the deepest north of Italy, where the sea is, more than anything else, an abstraction— there also surfaced words from my dialect, Sicilian. The ten years he'd spent in Sicily for work had left traces upon him. For an instant, the sounds of the south took possession of that gigantic body, dominating him. Then the moment would come to an end and he'd run out of things to say and just stare at me, in all his majesty, like a mountain of the north.

He'd become a diver practically by sheer chance, a shot at a job that he'd jumped at immediately after completing his military service.

"We divers are used to dealing with death, from day one they told us it would be something we'd encounter. They tell us over and over, starting on the first day of training: People die at sea. And it's true. All it takes is a single mistake during a dive and you die. Miscalculate and you die. Just expect too much of yourself and you die. Underwater, death is your constant companion, always."

He'd been called to Lampedusa as a rescue swimmer, one of those men on the patrol boats who wear bright orange wetsuits and dive in during rescue operations.

He told me just how tough the scuba diving course had been, lingering on the mysterious beauty of being underwater, when the sea is so deep that sunlight can't filter down that far and everything is dark and silent. The whole time he'd been on the island, he'd been doing special training to make sure he could perform his new job at an outstanding level.

He said: "I'm not a leftist. If anything, the complete opposite."

His family, originally monarchists, had become Fascists. He, too, was in tune with those political ideas.

He added: "What we're doing here is saving lives. At sea, every life is sacred. If someone needs help, we rescue them. There are no colors, no ethnic groups, no religions. That's the law of the sea."

Then, suddenly, he stared at me.

He was enormous even when he was sitting down.

"When you rescue a child in the open sea and you hold him in your arms..."

And he started to cry, silently.

His arms were still folded across his chest.

I wondered what he could have seen, what he'd lived through, just how much death this giant across the table had faced off with.

After more than a minute of silence, words resurfaced in the room. He said that these people should never have set out for Italy in the first place, and that in Italy the government was doing a bad job of taking them in, wastefully and with a demented approach to issues of management. Then he reiterated the concept one more time: "At sea, you can't even think about an alternative, every life is sacred, and you have to help anyone who is in need, period." That phrase was more than a mantra. It was a full-fledged act of devotion.

He unfolded his words slowly, as if they were careful steps down the steep side of a mountain.

"The most dangerous situation is when there are many vessels close together. You have to take care not to get caught between them because, if the seas are rough, you could easily be crushed if there's a collision. I was really in danger only once: There was a force-eight gale, I was in the water with my back to a refugee boat loaded down with people, and I saw the hull of our vessel coming straight at me, shoved along by a twenty-five-foot wave. I moved sideways with a furious lunge that I never would have believed I could pull off. The two hulls crashed together. People fell into the water. I started swimming to pick them up. When I returned from that mission, I still had the picture of that hull coming to crush me before my eyes. I sat there on the edge of the dock, alone, for several minutes, until I could get that sensation of narrowly averted death out of my mind."

He explained that when you're out on the open water, the minute you reach the point from where the call for help was launched, you invariably find some new and unfamiliar situation.

"Sometimes, everything purrs along smoothly, they're calm and quiet, the sea isn't choppy, it doesn't take us long to get them all aboard our vessels. Sometimes, they get so worked up that there's a good chance of the refugee boat overturning during the rescue operations. You always need to manage to calm them down. Always. That's a top priority. Sometimes, when we show up on the scene, the refugee boat has just overturned, and there are bodies scattered everywhere. Africans, for some physical reason, maybe because they lack significant amounts of body fat, tend to sink much faster. So, you have to work as quickly as you can. There is no standard protocol. You just decide what to do there and then. You can swim in a circle around groups of people, pulling a line to tie them together and reel them in, all at once. Sometimes, the sea is choppy and they'll all sink beneath the waves right before your eyes. In those cases, all you can do is try to rescue as many as you can."

There followed a long pause, a pause that went on and on. His gaze no longer came to rest on the wall behind me. It went on, out to some spot on the Mediterranean Sea that he would never forget.

"If you're face-to-face with three people going under and twenty-five feet farther on a mother is drowning with her child, what do you do? Where do you head? Who do you save first? The three guys who are closer to you, or the mother and her newborn who are farther away?"

It was a vast, boundless question.

It was as if time and space had curved back upon themselves, bringing him face-to-face with that cruel scene all over again.

The screams of the past still resonated.

He was enormous, that diver.

He looked invulnerable.

And yet, inside, he had to have been a latter-day Saint Sebastian, riddled with a quiverful of agonizing choices.

"The little boy is tiny, the mother extremely young. There they are, twenty-five feet away from me. And then, right here, in front of me, three other people are drowning. So, who should I save, then, if they're all going under at the same instant? Who should I strike out for? What should I do? Calculate. It's all you can do in certain situations. Mathematics. Three is bigger than two. Three lives are one more life than two lives."

And he stopped talking.

Outside the sky was cloudy, there was a wind blowing out of the southwest, the sea was choppy. I thought to myself: Every time, every single time, I have the distinct sensation that I'm face-to-face with human beings who carry an entire graveyard inside them.

I TRIED CALLING my uncle Beppe, my father's brother. We called each other pretty frequently. Often my uncle would ask me: "But why doesn't my brother ever call me?"

I'd answer: "He doesn't even call me, and I'm his first-born son, Beppuzzo, it's just the way he is."

The phone rang and rang for more than a minute, with no answer.

I hung up and went back inside.

We ate dinner, tuna cooked in sweet-and-sour onions and a salad of fennel, orange slices, and smoked herring.

There were four of us sitting around the table: Paola, Melo, my father, and me.

We were at Cala Pisana, at Paola's house. Paola is a friend of mine. She's a lawyer who's given up her practice and has lived on Lampedusa for years now. There, with her boyfriend Melo, she runs the bed and breakfast where I usually stay as my base of operations whenever I'm doing research on the island.

I was setting forth my considerations on that exceedingly long day, in a conversation with Paola. From time to time, Melo would nod, producing small sounds, monosyllabic at the very most. My father, on the other hand, made no sounds whatsoever. He was the silent guest. Patiently, with his gaze turned directly to the eyes of whoever was speaking, he displayed a considerable ability to listen that he'd developed in the forty-plus years he'd practiced his profession, cardiology. He invited people to tell him things just by the way he held his body.

I was considering out loud that everything happening on Lampedusa went well beyond shipwrecks, beyond a simple count of the survivors, beyond the list of the drowned.

"It's something bigger than crossing the desert and even bigger than crossing the Mediterranean itself, to such a degree that this rocky island in the middle of the sea has become a symbol, powerful and yet at the same time elusive, a symbol that is studied and narrated in a vast array of languages: reporting, documentaries, short stories, films, biographies, postcolonial studies, and ethnographic research. Lampedusa itself is now a container-word: migration, borders, shipwrecks, human solidarity, tourism, summer season, marginal lives, miracles, heroism, desperation, heartbreak, death, rebirth, redemption, all of it there in a single name, in an impasto that still seems to defy a clear interpretation or a recognizable form."

Papà had remained silent the whole time. His blue eyes were a well of still water in whose depths you could read no judgment whatsoever.

Paola had just poured herself an espresso.

"Lampedusa is a container-word," she repeated under her breath, nodding to herself more than to me.

She sugared her coffee and went on with her thoughts.

"And in a container, sure enough, you can put anything you like."

Little by little, with a gradual rising tone, her voice grew louder, and the pace of her words became increasingly relentless.

"In the container called Lampedusa, you really can fit everything and the opposite of everything. Take the Center where the young people are brought after they land. Do you remember? You saw it when you came back here the year after the Arab Spring."

It was the summer of 2012 and I'd asked a few Lampedusan *picciriddi*—kids—who I'd met on the beach: "Do you all ever go to the Center?" I was fantasizing about the idea that the structure where anyone who landed on Lampedusa was taken must somehow constitute a focus of enormous fascination for them. *"E che ci ham'a iri a fare?"* those children had replied in dialect. I was stunned to hear their answer: "Why on earth would we bother with that place?" I had been convinced, until that moment, that the presence of new arrivals must have generated a monstruous well of curiosity, becoming the sole topic of conversation, of play, of adventure. Something rooted in the epic dimension.

"Would you take me there?" I'd asked them, hesitantly, already anticipating my defeat.

"We'd rather die."

There was nothing about the Center that appealed to them, it had never interested them. Only after I finally saw it did I understand that I had committed an enormous mistake: I'd interacted with the children but used the parameters of an adult. Along the road that leads to the Center, there was nothing but rocks, brushwood, and dry-laid stone walls upon which signs appeared here and there, reading FOR SALE. The only form of life was a thunderous bedlam of crickets. It was an arid place. Of course the *picciriddi* never went there, there was nothing fun to do, nowhere to play. Myths aren't built out of nothing.

The Center had been built from the ground up on the site of an old army barracks. A number of dormitory structures, an open plaza, an enclosure fence. For all intents and purposes, it looked like a prison.

"Has anything changed about the Center in the last few years?" I asked Paola.

"The name. At first it was called the Temporary Settlement Center, then the Center for Identification and Expulsion, and now it's a Hot Spot Center, whatever that's supposed to mean. The governments change, the names rotate, but the structure is always the same: Under normal conditions it can hold 250 people, in an emergency situation it could take in at the very most 381 full-time residents. Those are the numbers, you can't increase the number of bathrooms, or, for that matter, the number of beds. And in 2011 more than two thousand people were packed in there, for days and days, without being told at all what was to become of them. The world applauded the Arab Spring, and then imprisoned its protagonists. Was this the best response we could provide to their demands? And do you know what you create by keeping too many people shut up in such a small space? Rage. That's how you create wild animals. And, in fact, a revolt broke out; they burned their mattresses and set fire to one wing of the structure."

My father listened impassively, even though—clearly listening, but remaining opaque, inscrutable—he had to be squirreling away all that information. Melo was chewing on his lower lip, Paola continued to talk without taking her eyes off the demitasse of espresso.

"The Center, at least on paper, is supposed to be a containment facility if nothing else, right? And in fact, there's a hole in the fence around the Center. I think it dates back to that period in 2011, but I couldn't rule out by any means that the hole was there even earlier. It's a great big hole and it works as a pressure valve, in fact, allowing the young men to get out, take a walk, come into town to try to get in touch with their families by using the Internet through the generosity of a number of residents. And what are you going to do, if a little kid asks you to let him talk to his mother to let her know that he's still alive? Tell him he can't use your computer?"

She'd continued to stir her espresso, tiny spoon in little demitasse. The sound of steel rattling against porcelain had punctuated the cadence of her words, like a rhythmic counterpoint, necessary to keep from losing the thread, to keep from plummeting body and soul into an abyss of screaming.

"Believe me, Davidù, it's a good thing that hole is there. It's a door, a way of keeping them from feeling like caged animals. So, you see what the point is? The Center is a structure garrisoned by the police force, inside which no one can go without special authorization. Not even a priest can go in. The facade remains intact. But in the fence, there's always been a hole. It's a well-known fact and no one does anything about it. And it's a good thing that no one does anything about it, let me say that for the thousandth time. Here is a concrete example of how closely emergency and hypocrisy have to coexist, bureaucracy and solidarity, common sense and cult of appearances. Lampedusa is a container of opposites, for real."

Through the open window came the roar of waves, water rising, tumbling, crashing down onto the sand, pouring back out, and starting over again, in an endless relaunching. Melo, seated at the head of the table, had consigned himself to silence, just like my father. Melo, too, spoke little if at all, the whole day through, at most a bare handful of words, often drawled out, because speaking costs effort and effort is a burden.

Paola sipped her coffee slowly, and it wasn't until she'd finished it that she started talking again.

"It is History that's taking place, Davidù. And History is complicated, a mosaic full of tiles of different shapes and sizes, sometimes similar, other times diametrically opposed, yet all of them necessary in order for the final picture to emerge. No, wait, let me correct myself: It's not that History's taking place now. It's been taking place for twenty years."

She started taking long drags on a cigarette, her third in half an hour.

"As you had an opportunity to understand yourself this morning, the scale of this event can be perceived immediately when you witness a landing. But even if someone never had a chance to witness one, what can you expect them to care about the history of your, my, our perceptions? History is already determining the course of the world, tracing out the future, structurally modifying the present. It's an unstoppable movement. And this time, History is sending people ahead, in flesh and blood, people of every age. They set sail across the water, they land here. Lampedusa isn't an exit, it's a leg in a longer journey."

She crushed her cigarette out in the ashtray while Melo poured himself what beer remained in the bottle. Through the open window, warm fall air pushed into the room, scented with hot sand and salt-sea brine.

In the days following the Arab Spring, mass arrivals had begun on the shores of Lampedusa. An island resident named Piera had happened to be down at Porto Nuovo, or New Port, to supervise the efforts of the town constables.

"I've still got the scene before my eyes, it was completely insane! So many people had landed that you couldn't make your way through the port. They were everywhere, the wharf was packed and the vessels were coming in and landing, more people one right after the other. A procession of refugee boats! And they were coming ashore by the thousands! We were there to give them a hand, but we were hardly prepared for anything like those numbers. A carabiniere was telling all the new arrivals in French to move over to the hill to make room for the others, and in the meantime new boats were coming in from the sea, all of them packed to the gunwales, and there was just no time to move people aside before the new refugee boats had already landed more young people. I really couldn't begin to guess how many thousands came in that afternoon, it was impossible to count them, seven thousand, eight thousand, nine thousand, there was no settled number. And how could we ever reckon that number? There were more of them than there were islanders on Lampedusa, that much is certain. The ones who were standing on the hill, as soon as the boats came in carrying their families—wives, husbands, children—would rush down to rejoin their loved ones. An incredibly crazy scene: The police would try to separate them and we were caught in the middle, knocked back and forth. You couldn't figure out what was going on. And from the sea, boat after boat kept arriving, so many of them, in quick succession. A flotilla! No one had ever seen such a thing. There was a gentleman who arrived with a falcon on his arm. On another refugee boat, one young Tunisian had brought his own sheep. A lovely sheep! A breed of sheep I'd never seen in my life, spectacular. A thick coat of wool, very curly! Stupendous. But in the end, we had to put the animal down. There was no alternative."

There were more foreigners than residents on Lampedusa, more than ten thousand refugees as compared to five thousand islanders. Fear and curiosity coexisted with mistrust and pity. The shutters remained fastened tight, or else they'd open to hand out sweaters and shoes, electric adapters to charge cell phones, glasses of water, a chair to sit on, and a seat at the table to break bread together. These were flesh-and-blood people, right there before our eyes, not statistics you read about in the newspapers or numbers shouted out over the television. And so, in a sort of overtime of aid and assistance, people found and distributed ponchos because it was raining out, or they cooked five pounds of pasta because those young people were hungry and hadn't eaten in days.

Everyone had been abandoned to their own devices.

The following year, the Italian government proudly proclaimed the figure of "zero landings on Lampedusa" as if it were a medal of honor to be pinned to its chest.

"And it's true," Paola had assured me that summer in 2012. "No boats are landing here anymore. We didn't even see any in the spring. And do you know why? When the refugee boats are intercepted they're escorted all the way to Sicily, and that's where the landings take place, far out of the spotlight. Which means: zero landings on Lampedusa. From a purely statistical point of view, the logic is impeccable. And yet, you see? The island is fragmented, in the throes of anxiety, tumbled and tossed in this media maelstrom, a hail of contradictions. People talk less and less and, when they do, it's only to complain about concrete problems, such as the lack of a hospital, for instance, or the cost of gasoline, which here is the highest in all of Italy. And they point out, with a touch of bitterness, that all the attention is always focused on those who arrived over the water, while the everyday challenges that we residents face don't really seem to matter to anyone, except to us."

There was the vacation season, the real engine of the island's economy, to get up and running.

From time to time, someone would shoot a furtive glance toward the horizon.

"Sooner or later, something will come back to these beaches," a fisherman had told me. That prediction, shared by all the residents, came true the following year, on October 3, 2013. It was an event that outpaced even our wildest nightmares. A refugee boat overturned just a few hundred yards off the coast of the island, the waters filled up with corpses, and Lampedusa was overrun by coffins and television news crews. What had actually changed in the recent years, after all, were just the minor details. The corpses found in the fishing nets, for example, were simply tossed back into the sea in order to prevent the fishing boats from being confiscated and held in a subsequent investigation. The reports of alleged sinkings—alleged because the only sources were the words of those who had traveled on sister refugee boats—were only mentioned at the tail end of the newscasts. In the absence of a corpse, it's always better to leave death confined to territories that everyone prefers not to explore. And yet, in the months that preceded the October tragedy, the everyday rescue work carried out by the Italian Coast Guard continued as always, people continued to trek across the Sahara, women continued to be raped in Libyan prisons, the refugee boats and the rubber dinghies set sail and were intercepted, or else they sank.

History certainly hadn't stopped.

"How long have you been in this house?" my father asked Paola and Melo, breaking the silence that had come to shroud the room. I whipped my head around to look at him. A chill ran up my back. At first glance, Papà's physical posture remained unchanged: He was still seated with his legs crossed, his arms folded across his chest, his brow smooth and unfurrowed. But farther down, you could see the slightest hint of a dance in his foot on the floor. His trouser cuff, on a line with his ankle, was vibrating almost imperceptibly; if you looked up even as far as his knee, that tiny motion had already disappeared. I knew very well that drumming of the foot, oh how I knew it: That was my movement, too, my foot did the same thing, precisely when I was about to intuit something.

This was the beginning of a running start.

As an understanding of the things that had happened grew closer, it would increase the frequency of that drumming.

I looked at Papà.

Were we really so similar, he and I?

Did our bodies speak the same language?

Perhaps he, too, when anguish was devouring him, could feel his breath crashing into his ribs.

Paola had started to answer, lighting up her fourth cigarette.

"The earliest documentation of this house is a photo from 1957 that depicts it as it was then: an old ice plant, no longer in use. The photo was taken by my father in the days when he first fell in love with Cala Pisana. Papà had escaped here to Lampedusa because he'd originally fallen head over heels in love with a place in Libya, where he worked, near the archaeological digs of Sabratha. He'd always tell us about that beautiful beach with the palm trees that ran all the way down to the sea, and he so desperately wanted to have a house there. His friends and acquaintances talked him out of it immediately, though: 'Don't buy anything in Libya, the political situation is too complicated, there's no security, you'd always worry they might just nationalize everything and then they'd expropriate your house. What's more, you and your family would be at risk. But, seeing that you like these landscapes, why don't you go take a trip to Lampedusa?'"

I don't know why I'd never asked Paola about her past.

So often, this is what happens: You search far away when instead you ought to begin your investigation with what's close at hand.

Paola went on smoking and talking freely.

"Back then, my father hardly knew whether Lampedusa was even part of Italy, he'd never heard of the place. Anyway, he came to the island and fell in love with it. The old industrial plant went bankrupt and was put up for auction. My father bought it on March 8, 1966, exactly a year before I was born, even though during those nine years, from 1957 in the first photo until the year he bought it, my father had continued to come back to the island, at times alone, at times with my mother. This house was absolutely the first house on Lampedusa built by a nonresident. The renovation work was completed in 1973. We've lived in it since then, even though, during the years of the renovation, we still continued to come here—me, Papà, Mamma, and my brother—sleeping in fishermen's houses and in the only hotels they had here back then, which were few in number. We saw every inch of the island before we finally slept in our own house."

Melo rolled himself a cigarette that he didn't light, leaving it teetering on the edge of the table, the filter sticking out in midair, the part with the tobacco on the tablecloth. My father, beside me, continued moving his feet at the same pace as before.

Paola, her back still turned to the water, went on with her story.

"On summer evenings, we'd go down to the town, the grown-ups would stop at the café to get something to drink while me and my brother would play with asphalt bricks that we took from the construction work underway on Via Roma. Everywhere you looked was pounded dirt—the streets weren't paved—and we'd build ourselves a little playhouse using those black bricks. We were building our island. We spent the summer playing with the other kids, all of them Lampedusan, because while the grown-ups might go off to the Guitgia, Cala Pisana is the favorite beach of the children of Lampedusa and always has been. What's more, right in front of the house are the Testa di Polpo, the Octopus Head rocks. In those years, I began one of my closest friendships, with Simone: We spent endless hours diving off those rocks."

Simone was a fixed point of reference in the lives of Paola and Melo. They had spent vast amounts of time together. Simone had told me so in no uncertain terms: "To me, at the beginning, Paola was Paolo. And not because she was mannish in appearance, but precisely because she played all the same games as we *màsculi*. We'd jump headfirst off the rocks, and she'd jump headfirst right alongside of us. We'd jump off the Octopus Head and so would she, just the same. We'd fight, we'd wrestle, we'd shove, and she was always there, right with us. I only realized that she was a female when, as we grew, around the age of ten, she started to take the shape of a woman. Our friendship goes back practically our whole lives. I remember that when she and Melo became a couple, the first time I went to see them in Palermo, Melo was practically saying: '*Ma chisto chi bòle?*' What did I think I wanted? But it was almost as if he was the intruder, so strong and wonderful the ties of friendship were between her and me." Simone had also explained to me the initiation rites of the *picciriddi* on the island. One of those took place right in Cala Pisana and it involved diving *a capuzzùni*, headfirst, off the Octopus Head rocks. The age when you were expected to take on that challenge: six years old. Height of the rocks: almost twenty-five feet. The second rite of passage, on the other hand, took place at the Guitgia beach. There you had to free dive. On the right of the beach there was a patch of *Posidonia* seagrass and you had to swim out to it, remaining underwater the whole way. If you could hold your breath all the way out to the patch of *Posidonia* seagrass, then you weren't a little kid anymore. You'd start trying to do it when you were about nine. Distance from the beach to the patch of *Posidonia* seagrass: about two hundred feet.

"On Lampedusa, the children aren't *picciriddi*, they're fish," Simone had said with a laugh. And it was true. He'd become a professional scuba diver. Over the last few summers, though, he'd almost never had a chance to see Paola and Melo. Working as an underwater instructor, he was constantly out on boats, morning and afternoon. All the same, in spite of the fact that in the summer they were unable to spend as much time together as they would have liked, Simone was still a tangible presence in my friends' home, and he continued to pop up in the stories they told.

Paola took a long drag on her cigarette, blew out a plume of smoke with determined slowness, then went on talking.

"In 1993 my father retired and he moved here permanently, making this his official residence. Basically, this was his life: In the summer, he'd have friends come to visit, in the winter he'd close up the house and travel around Italy as their guest. Trieste, Madonna di Campiglio, the Cinque Terre. My father died at the end of August 2002, after a protracted illness. I remained close to him, stuck in Palermo taking care of him. That September Melo and I returned to the island. We had an idea: move here to live and start a bed and breakfast as a source of income. I really couldn't stand working as a lawyer in Palermo anymore. As soon as we landed, I remember clear as day, we went by the

Bar dell'Amicizia for some breakfast, and who came over to say hello? My friend Simone. He was with two young couples. He asked us right away: 'Hey, these friends are looking for a place to stay, what should we do? Can you take them?' Melo and I said yes. That was our first experience running a B&B, thanks to Simone. We charged them ten thousand lire a day per room. But the house, when we first got here, was a real wreck. After that summer, we didn't come back again until Christmas. Moving to Lampedusa would basically have meant giving up everything else. Those were days when we did a lot of thinking. Then this thing happened, I swear to you, this is the truth. It was morning, I was sitting on the toilet and thinking: I want to move forward with this decision, but I need a sign, something that would tell me: 'Move to Lampedusa!' And then, all of a sudden, the rubber tubing on the bidet right in front of me split open, drenching me completely. I was dripping with water. I couldn't even call out to Melo because the spray was so strong. Fine. I made up my mind that that was the sign, that was my home telling me: 'Come fix me, because I'm dying.' I walked out of the bathroom wet as a hen and I told Melo: 'Okay, the rubber tubing broke, let's move to Lampedusa.' I went right back to Palermo alone, Melo stayed here to fix up the house."

Now that he'd been called into the discussion, Melo could hardly refrain from offering his version of events. He started by exhaling forcefully, as if pumping himself up before beginning to speak. For some Palermitans, the act of speaking seems to demand so much effort that a preliminary warm-up is required: lungsful of air, a sonorous expansion of the ribs, movement of nostrils, lips, and neck. Then Melo spoke, maintaining a low, steady tone of voice. After all, it was already a big deal that he was uttering words, we could hardly expect that on top of that he'd also turn up the volume.

"I came to Lampedusa absolutely without thinking, just to accompany Paola. I felt no special attraction to the island. Starting with that Christmas in 2002, I stayed on Lampedusa for a year and a half without leaving. The house was reduced to little more than a bare shell, we needed to fix it all. Finding qualified builders on the site was really impossible, though, and in any case, it would have cost us ten times the money we had. So I stayed behind to do the first renovation work myself. I wound up using lots of material that came in from the sea, especially wood. The main beam that runs over the front door, for instance, is one of those beams they have in harbors lined with truck tires so that ships can bump against them safely when they moor. A few especially nice planks, which had washed in to shore, on the other hand, we incorporated into the kitchen."

Melo seemed exhausted. He'd spoken, it was clear that he now needed coffee. Paola picked up on that request, stood up, turned on the burner, and set down the second espresso pot of the evening. The new round of coffee was about to begin. Papà appeared appreciative, a faint smile had begun to flicker around the left side of his mouth. Melo made a further effort and finally lit the cigarette that he'd left tee-tering on the edge of the table.

Years ago, one afternoon when we were both sitting on the sofa watching the TV that was always on with the sound permanently turned off in the dining room, Melo had told me about a number of stories from his life before meeting Paola. Among the many jobs that he had had—cook, technician for the Compagnia Ligure Oceanografica Energetica, restaurateur—his work as a skipper was what he had done for the longest time and had made him happiest. The summer he was supposed to take his own boat from the Aeolian Islands to Capri—it was September 1984 and there were three of them on the boat, him and two friends—he had run into a terrible storm on the Tyrrhenian Sea, so bad that it sank the boat. A genuine shipwreck, with water pouring in and the hull sinking straight to the bottom of the sea. His motorcycle had been on board, too. It's still resting on the seabed somewhere. Melo and his two friends jumped over-board in great haste, taking with them everything they were able to gather in time: the little dinghy, of course, a blanket to use as a sail, life jackets, a few cans of tuna, and lots of cans of beer, which they drank the whole time they were lost at sea. In the terror of those moments, Melo even managed to grab the keys to his motorcycle.

"To tell the truth, I'd mistaken the keys for a pack of cigarettes," he admitted with a laugh. "Nothing made any sense, there was water coming in from above and from below, from right and from left, the boat was going down, and I had no intention of spending days on end without a smoke. But instead..."

After two days on the open seas, they sighted land. There were only rocks and brushwood. They abandoned their little dinghy and started walking. It was evening, the wind was blowing, and they were practically naked and drenched to the bone. After an hour, they saw a light: a big hotel. They ran and pounded loudly on the door. The night clerk came to answer and found himself face to face with these three individuals in their underwear and life jackets. "Excuse us, but where are we?" they all asked in unison. "Settefrati," the man replied. Settefrati! They were in the province of Palermo, the current had carried them a long distance in the opposite direction.

"That was the last time that me and my two friends were together: on a rubber dinghy drifting across the Mediterranean. Since then, the three of us have never once been in the same place," Melo concluded, as if for the first time, in that exact precise moment, he was becoming aware of that fact.

As he told his story, we all laughed and laughed.

Paola had taken the espresso pot off the flame and brought it to the table. She poured a round of coffee into the dark blue enameled demitasse cups. At the center of the table was the sugar. Paola and Melo added sugar to their coffee, my father and I didn't. You could hear in that lovely evening silence the sound of the waves washing back out and, intermittently, the shrill cry of the shearwaters. Paola lit her fifth cigarette and smoked the whole thing. Melo collected the espresso cups, rinsed them in the sink, and came back to the table. Paola was looking out the window. Melo, too, turned to stare out to sea. Both their gazes had come to rest at a specific point in the cove, fairly close to shore, about twenty yards from the window, if that.

My foot started drumming very fast.

"What are you looking at?" I asked. It really was as if that question had originated down under the table, out of that movement of flesh against the floor. My father's foot had also perceptibly quickened its pace. We were playing on the same team, and we hadn't even realized it. We were beating time together, devoted to the same objective: to hear the next words out of Paola and Melo's mouths. This was the goal to which Papà's initial question had been directed, a question that had been meant to prepare the ground, knock down the defenses, train the voice to name the past.

Once again turning her back to the sea, Paola took another cigarette, lit it, and smoked it, staring at it insistently, as if searching for the right words in the swirls of the smoke as it rose from her hands: a circle, an elongation, at last, a dismembering.

"I'll never be able to erase the scene from my memory. I was sitting in front of the television watching *L'isola dei Famosi*. Melo was at the desk doing something on his computer. It was raining. At a certain point, we hear voices. Lots and lots of voices. I get up, walk out into the darkness and the rain, and I see an indeterminate, enormous number of people coming up out of the water. I immediately say to Melo: 'It's a landing.' We look each other right in the eye and we say to each other: 'Let's lock the doors and windows.' And at the exact instant in which we hear ourselves uttering these words, I say: 'But what the fuck are we saying? Let's go give them a hand.' And we went outside."

She stubbed her cigarette out in the ashtray. She looked at her hands and fingers, as if she could find the past there, caught under her nails, still not free to go its way once and for all.

It was Melo who took up the tale.

"It was dark as pitch out and we couldn't produce enough light to see with our flashlights, so I drove the car down to the beach, as close as I could get, with the headlights on bright to get as much light as possible, so that these people could get things figured out a little better. The rubber dinghy had stranded and they were piling out into the waves to make their way to shore. Paola was much better in that situation than I was because she has a quick, ready mind: While I was helping people get out of the rubber dinghy, she noticed a young man lying face down on the beach, completely submerged in salt water. I remember that scene clear as day: Paola going down to the far-right corner of the cove, grabbing this kid, and pulling his head out of the water. I really think she saved his life."

Melo didn't change his tone of voice. He went on talking as if he were just describing the route to follow when you sail from Palermo to Ustica.

"In those days, people who reached Lampedusa would perform a very strange action that they no longer do now. When they would reach the island on their vessel, they'd immediately dismount the outboard engine from the rubber dinghy—it's easy and quick to dismount it, you only have to unscrew a couple of wing nuts—and then they'd throw it in the water to make sure it could no longer be used. They explained that they did it because they were terrified at the thought that someone might order them: 'Turn around and go back to where you came from.' That night I saw them do that very same thing. It really made quite an impression on me. I knew no one would dream of telling them to go back to where they came from, especially not in those conditions. They really were terrified. Immediately afterward, they started searching for things in the dinghy, maybe their identity papers, maybe their money, who knows what, really, there was no light, you could barely see a thing, and everyone was so panicky and upset. When they got back to shore, I realized that some of them had immediately changed their clothes. I don't remember any old people. There were certainly children, young people, and adults. There was also one tiny little baby. He was in an improvised cradle that we pulled out of the rubber dinghy and carried to shore."

Melo pointed out to the patio, which was directly behind my father and me.

"None of them were willing to come in. They stayed out on the patio, no matter how often we invited them in. It wasn't cold out, being outdoors or indoors practically amounted to the same thing. We'd emptied the larder because they were starving. Dying of thirst, more than anything else. We also found them some clothing, jackets for the most part, and blankets and beach towels to dry off with."

Paola had emerged from her silent confab with her own hands. She, too, was staring at the patio. She came in on the wake of Melo's last words.

"They weren't willing to come inside because they were all wet and dirty. They didn't want to make a mess. While they were getting dried off and eating and drinking on the patio, I phoned down to the Capitaneria di Porto, or port authorities, to alert them. There might have been forty of them... forty-four, forty-five... that was the standard number of people back then that they loaded onto a rubber dinghy. We had to wait, I don't know how long, half an hour, an hour, and then they came down and got them. And that's that."

The story seemed to have come to an end, but Paola went on, her gaze resting on the patio.

"I never saw those kids again."

Her fingers were intertwined. Her hands, now lying on the table, almost seemed to be propping her up.

"Have you come to terms with what was going on?" my father asked. His foot had fallen still again.

It was Melo who replied.

"We've come to terms with the fact that we, too, could see what was going on," he said. He'd resumed breathing sonorously, a sign that the fuel powering his words would soon run out.

"There was no mistaking the fact that something was going on. But that the landings were taking place at the port was, up until then, another matter. Because if they came from the west, they were more likely to land on the beaches farther west. Instead, here we're farther east and in front of our house, behind the endless sea, we know that after about six hundred fifty miles you'll hit Cyprus, but between here and Cyprus there's absolutely nothing. Now, if you're sailing from the west, you'd expect a landing on the beaches of that side of the island. To land here is off course, a landing here would be an exceptional event. Which over the years, however, has happened other times."

He pulled a cigarette out of Paola's pack and put it in his mouth without bothering to light it.

"No, I really never expected them to arrive on this beach. It was a technical problem, for me: Why sail all the way to here if they could land so many hours earlier on a beach farther west?"

He picked up the lighter and brought it close to his mouth.

"Basically, though, I'm a sailor, a man of the sea, and to me one rescue is the same as any other, here or on the open water, it makes no difference."

He snapped the flame into life, pushed the cigarette closer to it, inhaled, put down the lighter, and exhaled smoke.

"I'm sorry I can't be any more exhaustive."

He'd said absolutely all he meant to say.

Paola released her fingers from their reciprocal embrace and looked us in the eyes again.

She wasn't done talking.

"I think that the most traumatic aspect was the fact that we were afraid. I carry the feeling of fear that I experienced with a great sense of shame, even though afterward I reprocessed it, telling myself: 'Okay, it's normal, it's human, the important thing is to get over it.' Still, we're ashamed of it, Melo and I, because we felt that fear. It really lasted just a moment, just a fleeting moment. But the first instinctive reaction was that: me saying, 'Let's lock ourselves inside.' I'll never forget it. What flashed before me was everything I'd ever said until then but which, when push came to shove, I wasn't doing at all."

She burst out laughing, loud and long.

"I was certainly preaching well, but I wasn't practicing what I preached, in the slightest. Even from before, I had my ideas as the left-wing intellectual that I was: You need to take people in, and you need not to be afraid of them. Then, the minute I actually found myself in the middle of them, fuck . . ."

That burst of laughter had been a liberation for her.

"A girlfriend of mine from Cantù, Loredana, had come here for the first time as our guest. She fell in love with the island and came back many times for work. She, too, was very open-minded, progressive, with left-wing ideas, you understand. Loredana worked as a hostess on a fairly large caïque, or sailboat. At night she'd sleep on board, anchored in the port, alone. One morning, just before dawn, she heard some strange sounds come from above, on deck. They were footsteps. Through the porthole she saw black legs. Lots and lots of black legs. What had happened? A refugee boat had arrived in port and had moored alongside the caïque because the wharf was too high, and so, in order to get up on the wharf, the young men were climbing onto the caïque, using it as a stepladder. Loredana told me that her first reaction was to lock herself in the cabin. After a moment, though, she thought to herself: 'Wait, what the fuck am I doing?' She opened the cabin, stepped out, and started helping the young refugees. When she told me about this, I recognized in her my own thought process. There exist two instincts—it's just that one precedes the other: self-protection and protecting your neighbor, because there's an instinct to help others, too. Fear of the Other, of the person you don't know, or whatever you don't know, whether it's a person, an animal, or something in nature, that's perfectly normal. And if you get over it the first time, it will probably not return. Or, at least, every time it returns, you're likely to have shorter and shorter reaction times; it will be easier and quicker to get over it. Every time that Loredana tells me about it, I recognize myself in her story: the same words, the same expressions, the same mixed emotions of shame and redemption, the same great indulgence in judging yourself."

Paola stood up. She was done. But there was still a piece missing from the puzzle. And it was a big fat piece. Melo had just gone to bed, it was past eleven, and all those words had tired him out so much that he'd needed to go lie down.

"When did the landing take place?" I asked her. My friend, usually so clearheaded and precise, admitted that she couldn't remember.

"I usually have a really good memory and I can keep a lot of information in my mind. But not this detail. I just can't remember."

She started looking around.

"It must have been before 2005, because the fact that we heard their voices from outside, the old frames must have still been in the windows. These new window frames are insulated. So it either happened in 2003 or else in 2004..."

She seemed sure of herself, but then, a second later, she came to a sudden halt and started backing up.

"No, hold on...it was 2004, because we moved in June 2003...but I was on the sofa watching TV, which means..."

She was struggling with her memory, drawing a blank.

There are traumas that can take decades to get over.

"I just can't seem to remember, for real. Still, I could tell you every movement I made and where Melo and I came together at the center of the living room when, looking each other in the eyes, we said to each other: 'Let's lock ourselves in.'"

She had acted out the whole scene: the gestures that she and Melo had exchanged, their respective positions in the room, the distance between their bodies, which increased and decreased while they gradually became aware of what was happening out there in the water, not twenty yards away from the back window, an awareness that bore in on them as a necessity. All that was lacking was the *when* to complete matters.

Paola sat back down, poured herself some more coffee, which was cold by now, added sugar, and drank it very slowly, exhausted by her recollections. Her voice, too, was tired, dropping an octave or two.

"All night long, I was terrified that I'd wake up the next morning and find some corpse in the light of day. In the darkness, it was impossible to say. That's always been my nightmare: How my relationship with this place might be changed, with this sea, with this house, with this landscape, if one day I happened to run into ... the tides bring in lots of things ... just now there's been a levant wind, and we need to go out and retrieve two wonderful pieces of wood that have beached here ... but if one day there should arrive here a ... I don't know ... I don't know ... I've never seen dead bodies. Ever. I've never wanted to come face-to-face with one."

She stood up from the table, said goodnight to us, and went after Melo.

Papà and I kissed each other on the cheeks, one peck per cheek, and went back to our respective rooms.

I found a text on my phone.

It was from Uncle Beppe.

It read: "Forgive me, I didn't have a chance to reply, I was so tired."

It was too late to call him back.

I got into bed and fell asleep instantly.

"YOU NEVER FORGET your first mass landing," those who had seen lots of them would say, half-serious, half in jest.

And they couldn't have been any more right about it.

It was November and it was morning.

The dinner at which Paola and Melo would tell us about that nighttime landing was later that day, that very evening.

My father and I had just landed on Lampedusa.

Our eyes were still virgin.

Rooted to the spot, I studied the scene of the people rescued in the open sea the night before by the Italian Coast Guard. Men, women, and children were all standing on the three patrol boats that were going to moor, one at a time, in order to carry out the landing operations.

There were so many of them.

I was on the Molo Favaloro wharf thanks to Paola, who had given me a badge from the Lampedusa Solidarity Forum, an association of secular and religious volunteers who were authorized to be on the wharf in order to monitor the landings. My father was just outside, beyond the wharf's iron gate.

As soon as we landed, Paola had come to the airport to pick us up and informed us, quite calmly, that there was going to be a landing any minute now.

"Do you want to see it with your own eyes, Davidù? That's why you came, isn't it?"

The volunteers had brought thermoses full of hot tea, they had stacks of thermal blankets to hand out, and they were unwrapping packs of cakes and cookies. I imitated everything they did.

The first of the Italian Coast Guard's three patrol boats approached the wharf. The men from the Red Cross and all the medical personnel were wearing gloves and masks. They shouted instructions and, before the eyes of the policemen in riot gear, the landing on the wharf began.

A couple of weeks earlier, in response to a sudden impulse, I asked my father to come with me to Lampedusa.

I'd never traveled anywhere alone with him before.

"Papà, what are you doing at the start of November?"

Ever since he'd retired, Papà had discovered a passion for photography. It had occurred to me that he might enjoy taking pictures of Lampedusa. I asked him over the phone, certain that he'd say no, and I waited, because that's the way it works when you talk to a southern Italian father: There has to be an ample parenthesis of silence before the answer, before any answer. It's a necessity, a matter of force majeure, it's as God commands. And in fact, after long, nerve-racking seconds, Papà's voice finally rang out at the other end of the line.

"Why, what are *you* doing at the start of November?"

He'd answered one question with another. A classic strategy out of medical case histories. I couldn't hope to compete with someone who'd practiced this profession for over forty years.

"I'm going back to Lampedusa, you've never seen the place, why don't you come with me?"

"But haven't you already been there?"

"Yes, lots of times."

More silence, interminable. On the phone with my father, no sound came to rescue me from that private emotional Siberia of mine. Then, just as the wolf appears on the snow, suddenly there was his voice again.

"How long would we stay there?"

"Five days, six at the most."

"And where would we stay?"

"Where I always go: my friend Paola's bed and breakfast. Separate rooms."

I imagined my father wandering around an infinitely vast room, without corners or walls.

"Can I pay with my debit card?"

"No, Papà, you can't. But you can always just wire the money from home before leaving."

Another silence, but this time with a different feeling to it: You could sense the gears grinding, his thoughts working their way through to their conclusions, his doubts finally resolved.

"Then I'll bring cash."

"Come on, then you're coming?"

"Yes."

The answer came promptly.

I wasn't ready for it.

There hadn't been the usual extended silence to warm it up.

What's more, my father had immediately started talking again.

"I want to bring my camera with me."

"That's why I decided to ask you to travel with me."

I dropped out those words one by one, in a low voice. My heart had started to race.

My father had changed his tone now. He was actually starting to sound a little giddy.

"It must be an interesting, stimulating place to photograph, though challenging, don't you think?"

He'd asked me an unexpected question. He'd asked my opinion. It caught me off-balance. So I decided to try his technique, and answered a question with another question.

"Papà, has your work as a cardiologist influenced the way that you take pictures?"

I was desperately trying to remain composed and dignified with him. And so my father also replied immediately.

"As the doctor that I am, I would put together lots of little clues until I could join them together and build a meaning out of them: a symptom, a sign, a laboratory data point. After all, the real work is this: adding together symptoms, signs, laboratory data points, in search of something that provides an explanation. There's a diagnostic hypothesis, and you go in search of what you hypothesized. In order to search, I have to have a gaze that can guide me, knowing what to look for and where to look for it. Modern-day medicine is a blind form of medicine, in-depth investigations tell us basically that doctors no longer know how to use their eyes. And doctors no longer know how to use their eyes because no one taught them how. But I was taught to use my eyes. My teacher, Professor Geraci, taught us the importance of using your eyes in medical analysis. So I'd say yes, my gaze has been influenced and at the same time trained by the profession I practiced. I bought a new lens recently, I can't wait to try it out. What do you say, should I bring my tripod?"

I wasn't ready for that hail of fatherly words.

I felt overwhelmed.

"Sure, sure, bring it," I stammered, hastily ending the conversation with a strange sensation, more or less like what it must have been to watch East Berlin awaken after the Wall came down.

In the south, we suffer from a lack of communication, which is the price we pay for our ancient culture with its belief that silence is a mark of manhood.

"*Omo di panza*"—literally, "man with a gut"—is the complimentary way we have of describing someone thought to have such a strong stomach that he can hold it all in: his doubts, his secrets, his traumas. It's a distinctive trait of paternalism: Remaining silent becomes an art that you learn from the earliest age. Speaking is the action of women, *una attività da fìmmina*. The weak talk, true macho men say nothing. The seal of silence, the threshold of that almost impregnable fortress that is omertà, is the *conditio sine qua non*, the indispensable prerequisite, for fitting in. In any case, just to be perfectly clear, *'a megghiu parola è chìdda ca 'un si dice*. The best word is the word you never said.

It is by no means strange that my father found in photography a medium that was particularly congenial to him as a form of expression. In this asphyxiating and, emotionally, almost illiterate setting, where the ability to name the things you desire is lacking, my papà's photos configure themselves as attempts to open out to a larger reality. His photos, in a certain sense, become the words that haven't been spoken. Taking pictures is the way that my father has finally found to speak aloud to himself, admitting his own helplessness concerning a given situation, or evaluating the scope of a failure, investigating deeply the reasons behind things, without any urgent need for an immediate response.

At the same time, photography also aspires to be something other than itself, becoming a symbol, filling in exactly those silences for which words aren't adequate.

The landing operations began with children only a few months old, the first to be taken out onto dry land. A man from the Italian Coast Guard held a little girl wrapped in a thermal blanket, so tiny she looked like a doll. His colleagues held him by the shoulders, making sure he didn't stumble and helping him to keep his balance, so that he was able to reach the wharf securely. Once he was on dry land, he handed the little girl to a nurse. The operation was performed rapidly and with painstaking care. The whole time the landing was underway, the man from the Italian Coast Guard looked the *picciridda* in the eyes. She was a sprout of three or maybe four months old, and he smiled at her the whole time.

Papà, is this the sense of gratification that you doctors feel when you save a child's life?

This was followed by the transfer of another *picciriddo*, a little boy only a few months old. Once again, it was as if we were watching the handoff of a crystal relay baton, so great was the care devoted to the handling of that tiny body. Inside a tent, the medical staff checked the health of the two babies. Then an adult left the boat. Just one. From sub-Saharan Africa. It was the father of the first child, the little girl. He went over to his daughter. He caressed her head with his forefinger and thanked anyone who met his gaze, bobbing his head in a series of bows. He was clenching his teeth to keep from bursting into tears. Father and daughter boarded the ambulance, along with a Red Cross volunteer who was carrying the other baby. They were all taken to the *Poliambulatorio*, or general hospital, for further examinations.

Then began the landing of the older children. They were five, six, seven, eight years old. Twenty or so of them. There was no need to carry any of them. They could walk on their own two legs. Except for two of them who wore heavy terry-cloth athletic socks instead of shoes, the kids were all barefoot. They wore brightly colored T-shirts, short pants, light dresses that ended above the knees. They tugged their thermal blankets close around them. A little girl started playing with hers: It had become a cape that, struck by the sunlight, emanated scales of light. Another *picciriddo* was so tired that he sat down on the ground, leaning his back against the low wall of the wharf and, closing his eyes, fell fast asleep.

"*Te ccà,*" Paola said to me. "Here." And she handed me a bag full of plush toys to hand out, along with the food, the tea, and the fruit juices. Each plush toy was a dinosaur made of purple cloth, about four or five inches tall, very soft. The frightened, bewildered procession of children was relieved by that gift of a small toy. The *picciriddi* focused all their attention on their toy. It was the key that opened a world of joy. None of them were crying. At times, they'd look around, uncertain where they were. They were all sub-Saharan. This was the first time they'd seen fair-skinned people, moored boats, toy purple dinosaurs. They drank their fruit juice and played silently. When the ambulance returned, they were taken to the Poliambulatorio. The ambulance had to make two trips. A volunteer from the Red Cross took the sleeping child in his arms and, exhausted, the child went on sleeping. It was eleven in the morning. The sirocco was blowing hard. The ambulance left, clearing space on the wharf, and the landing of the women and girls began.

The girls who landed were young, quite young, and very young. They were twenty years old, fifteen, twelve. On the wharf, the medical staff had begun routine operations to detect possible cases of scabies, checking each girl's hands.

The volunteers were smiling and joking around. Paola was talking with Alberto, a volunteer from Rome with a headful of dreadlocks.

"Sardines need to be cleaned with a steady, fine stream of water," she was explaining to him. "A quick slice with a knife and out come the innards, but you have to be quick, otherwise the sardine gets all drenched with water and the flavor of the sea disappears."

They were fooling around with the thermoses. Next to them, two volunteers were opening new packages of cookies and cakes. The hot tea was poured into plastic cups, then they had to wait for the medical personnel to give the young women permission to continue down the wharf toward the buses that were going to take them to the Center, and which had just pulled in through the metal gate. Suddenly, without warning, one of the young women fainted. She just slumped over and, in a single movement, dropped to the ground. The last residual bit of strength must have been used up, and the body had collapsed. The Red Cross staff hurried to her aid and laid her on a stretcher. She might have been fourteen or fifteen years old. Then a second girl fainted in much the same way, as if, truly, now that they were on dry land, the effort to survive might falter for a moment, just the time to take a rest, recharge, and then start again. The second girl was even younger, twelve at the most.

"They're dehydrated," I managed to pick up from the information that the physicians were exchanging between them.

Every time one of the young women passed out, it was experienced in silence. Then there were a third, a fourth, and even a fifth. The young women were loaded into an ambulance. It was as if five rocks had fallen into the lake of my heart. It was a matter of absorbing the pain, certainly, the same way that the waters swallow up the rocks. It's a matter of an instant, a fraction of a second in which everything seems to play out: the time of the impact, the sound of the water opening, the rock disappearing. But then, an instant later, something else ensues: The slow but unstoppable propagation of ripples across the lake in all directions, breaking against the shore, in a protracted lapping, inside the space of memory, with an imperceptible but systematic erosion of the shores of the heart.

The girls made it to the wharf, disembarking from the first and then the second patrol boat, while the third boat remained offshore, awaiting its turn. There were more than two hundred girls. They were confused and intimidated, like the children that they were. Some of them noticed the faintings, others didn't. There were no particular reactions at the sight of those falls. More than half of them were barefoot, the others wore flip-flops. None of them burst out sobbing, but a great many of them were choking back tears. The signal came for them to proceed toward the buses. Their motions were slow, their steps measured. It seemed like a procession, but in fact they were exhausted, at the limit of their strength.

The volunteers offered them cookies and cakes and hot tea. They said to each girl: "Welcome." The girls thanked them in low voices, *"Merci,"* "Thank you," a little bow, a faint smile. They held the tea with both hands, close to their faces, to warm themselves at its touch. More thermal blankets were distributed. Paola went around collecting the packaging of the cookies and cakes and the empty plastic cups. She'd talk with the girls: "Where do you come from?" *"D'où venez-vous?"* "Welcome," *"Bienvenue."*

She was smiling, as was Alberto, as were the other volunteers.

I was overwhelmed.

Paola came to my aid.

"Do you think that after everything they've been through, we can't welcome them with at least a smile? Come on, go get a thermos and pour some tea for the girls."

In the tent staffed by the medical personnel, the girls with signs of scabies between their fingers were being tended to. There were two of them. They were waiting for the ambulance to come back.

There was only one bus, and in order to take them all to the Center, it had to make four trips. While they were waiting, the girls leaned against the low wall. Some of them sat on the ground.

Only then did I realize that there wasn't even a portable toilet on the wharf.

"What about when it rains?" I asked Paola.

"We all get wet, us and them," she replied.

My father was hunched on a rock near the metal gate. He'd mounted the new lens on his camera.

Okay, I told myself, at least here's a serious reason not to burst into tears.

I couldn't cry in front of my father.

Not even if it killed me.

I distributed cookies and cakes and tea.

When all the girls had been taken to the Center, the men and boys stared coming ashore.

The first young men who set foot on dry land intoned a chant of thanksgiving, hands raised, foreheads raised to the sky after kissing the ground. Others sang in low voices. Some of them started to strike up a rhythm, softly clapping their hands. There were about three hundred of them and they were bone tired. For the most part, they wore track-suits and sweatshirts. Only a very few wore jackets. A dozen or so wore running shoes and sandals, a few had flip-flops, and there were others who had nothing on their feet but terry-cloth gym socks. Most of them were barefoot.

"These ones look plump and healthy, unlike the ones that came ashore the other day," noted a Red Cross volunteer.

Confused and silent, they went over to sit down against the low wall, doing their best to shade themselves against the sun.

The volunteers continued to distribute tea, cookies and cakes, and fruit juice.

I said, "Welcome," in English, to all the young men who had landed.

I tried talking to them, still in English of course.

"Where do you come from?"

"Niger," "Cameroon," "Syria," "Eritrea," "Sudan," "Somalia," "Morocco," "Tunisia," "Nepal."

The whole world, in other words.

"Hold on, what do you mean, Nepal?"

There were three of them. The only visa they'd been issued, even though there was a war raging there, had been for Libya. They'd left Nepal by boat, they'd reached India, they'd caught a plane to Tripoli, and from there, after a few weeks in prison, after paying the sum demanded, they'd set sail aboard that rubber dinghy for Europe.

Generally speaking, it costs more than two thousand dollars apiece to cross the Mediterranean.

The human trafficking industry is very powerful and also very profitable.

"It's nice here," one of the three Nepalese said.

He might have been twenty years old, maybe twenty-five, the same as his two friends.

"Where are we now?" he asked.

I explained to him that we were on the island of Lampedusa, the southernmost place in Europe.

"We are in Sicily right now. We are in Italy."

The young man bowed slightly in thanks. Then he asked again: "Are we in Europe?"

"Yes, we are. Welcome and good luck."

Next to us was a small group of young men who were more animated than the others. They were Moroccans, barely of age. Among them, one who must have been twenty astonished everyone because he spoke perfect Roman dialect.

"Che ce l'hai 'na sigaretta?" He asked for a cigarette.

Everyone was surprised: the volunteers, the cops, the Red Cross personnel.

"What is this? A migrant who speaks Roman dialect?"

At that moment I really wished that my father could be there to listen to that cadence, that dialect, that slurred, slightly chopped-off drawl that Romans have when they speak.

The boy told us that his father had Italian citizenship, as did his uncle. His folks had emigrated from Morocco when he was just a kid. He'd grown up on the outskirts of

Rome, and he'd lived there for fourteen years. He'd learned to read and write in Rome.

It was far too clear that that young man was Roman right down to the tips of his toes: the way he looked at you, the way he moved, the mixture of lightness and irony in his speech. He was truly Roman in a cultural sense. Not only did he speak dialect, he even gesticulated in Roman. That was his language, the structure of his thoughts.

Alberto, the Roman volunteer, asked him what quarter of Rome he was from.

"*Io so' de Tor Bella, tu?*" I'm from Tor Bella Monaca, what about you?

"*Prati, conosci?*" Prati, you know it?

"*E certo, ci ho fatto un rave.*" Sure, I went to a rave there.

In Rome he'd gotten married, too. He had a son he hadn't seen in two years because while he was still a minor he'd stolen a wallet, had been arrested, and after serving his time in prison, at the end of the trial, he'd been expelled from the country and sent back to Morocco.

"Who ever spoke a word of Arabic? Not me: I've spoken Italian all my life, I went to school here, only here. All around me were other kids speaking Arabic, and I couldn't understand a word! *Io nun capivo gnente.*" His plaintive conclusion was in pure *romanaccio*, the dialect of Rome.

He had tried to return to Italy by legal means, in particular by applying for a family reunification order.

"But at the embassy no one answers the phone, and at the consulate there's never anyone in the office. What little money I had, I spent it all on phone calls and failed attempts."

The waiting times were elephantine. So he started working as a bricklayer to earn enough to pay for a seat on a refugee boat. It took him two years, but he managed to scrape together the money needed. He'd set sail from Libya with the young men we were looking at.

"*Vojo rivedè mi moje e mi fijo.*" I want to see my wife and son again, he said, still in dialect.

He was smoking the cigarette that a volunteer had offered him. He seemed to be truly relieved now that he was back on dry land.

"The boat started taking on water when we were still just a couple miles away from the Libyan coast. The water came all the way up to our knees. Luckily, they came out to get us. *S'aa semo vista davero brutta.* It really got ugly there."

He smiled, took a drag on his cigarette, blew out a plume of smoke.

Suddenly, he changed expression, shrugging his shoulders.

"*Se me rimannano via, questa è la vorta che m'empicco davero.*" If they send me away, this is the time that I really hang myself after all.

The bus came back for the last load, picked up all the young people, and set off toward the Center again.

The Molo Favaloro was deserted now.

The total number of people who had landed was 523, including the *picciriddi*.

"All things considered, this was a pretty trouble-free landing, only five people passed out, no big deal."

"Is it usually worse, Paola?"

"It all depends on the conditions under which they take the crossing, Davidù. Sometimes they nearly all pass out, they're dehydrated and clinging to life by a thread, sometimes most if not all of them vomit on the wharf, and when they throw up all they're bringing up is gastric fluids, nothing more than that, so they need arms to support them and rags to clean faces and bodies. It depends. Lately the weather has been wonderful and the sea has been a nurturing father to them."

"But the things you all do—the hot tea, the cookies and cakes, the kind words of comfort, the purple plush toys—if it wasn't for you guys, nobody would do it at all, would they?"

Paola limited herself to shrugging her shoulders as she went to pick up the black trash bag full of dirty plastic cups and empty packages of cookies and cakes. Beyond the steel gate, my father was staring at the sea, his camera hanging around his neck and his hands in his pockets.

In his photographs, my father has a special predilection for focusing on minimal details. Rust, for instance, is something that especially appeals to him, or the corners of apartments where a single shadow line divides the interior into two parts, on one side sunlight filtering through a half-open window, on the other, darkness steeped in mystery.

One of his series that I love best is a collection of shots of colorful clothespins, portrayed like so many ballerinas suspended on a wire an instant before the curtain goes up.

My father is fascinated by the way that spaces and lines fit together and intersect, and he searches for those points of intersection while he observes a landscape, the corner of a house, a person's face.

When he's taking pictures of tumbledown houses with austere trees standing next to them, bare of leaves but still alive, what interests him is the equilibrium that is established between the subjects and the empty space that surrounds them.

He has a clinical eye, hence his affinity for the minimal detail that's capable of constructing a whole world of its own. This inclination of his is tied to his passionate love for the British poet T. S. Eliot, theorist of the objective correlative, whereby an object is symbolically charged with meaning and becomes something more than itself: a condition of grief, solitude, and grace.

There's something liturgical about the way he takes pictures. He reminds me of Cézanne. If he'd been a painter, he would have done mostly still lifes.

For an entire lifetime, Papà refused to fly. Now that he's retired, he's overcome his fear of flying. On the flight to

Lampedusa, sitting side by side, I tried to strike up a conversation by asking him why he started taking pictures. I only expected a few words, terse phrases, subject verb object, without adjectives or adverbs. But instead:

"My interest in photography sprang out of a memory: my father putting a camera into my hands. I was six years old. I still have that camera, it's the Voigtländer Vito C. It still works. Ten or so years after my father died, I remember that I was with your brother Marco and I said: I'd like to take a picture of this detail. Marco had a little compact camera he no longer needed, and he gave it to me."

Suddenly, it was as if Papà was no longer with me. He was immersed completely in his memories, scrutinizing his innermost self, naming hidden currents that generated emotional waves independent of his will.

He talked about himself and about his emotions with a lack of inhibition that I would have thought impossible.

He told me: "For me, taking pictures is a way of going on talking to my father."

I understood at that moment that he and my grandfather had loved each other much more dearly than I'd ever guessed, much more than their silence had suggested.

My father's words, poised, serene, blossomed from his mouth.

"When you get older you find yourself saying: 'Think of all the things I could have discussed with my father.' And so, continuing to walk with him, I take photographs, because photography is basically something you do on foot:

You have to walk, there aren't a lot of other options. You have to wander around, without looking for anything in particular, you already have what you want to photograph inside you. So, you can find what you're looking for a hundred yards from your front door or in Berlin at the monument to the victims of the Holocaust. And the whole time that I'm walking, I talk with my father."

His words were colors daubed onto the canvas without effort. It was then, for the first time, that I realized who my father was. He was at the same time my parent, my grandfather's son, and the adult orphan who, from the day of his bereavement on, was left with nothing but mourning and memories in order to build a relationship with his own father.

So that's why Papà takes so many photos of details, I thought to myself, he's showing these images to his own father. That's what touches me so deeply about it: There's the absolute painstaking care with which a child holds in his hand the object he's conquered in order to show it to his parent in exchange for a pat on the head, a loving word, a protective gaze, always, even long after death.

Such a visceral love, a love capable of transcending space, reaching beyond time.

I walked through the metal gate marked, "Military Zone, Entry Prohibited."

"What do you say, Papà?"

"About the landing?"

"Yes."

"Honestly, it was overwhelming."

We were walking along the port. The sirocco had sprung up for good now. It had encountered no obstacles along its path from the Sahara to here, and so it gleefully smacked us in the face with its hurtling grains of sand.

"I saw you put the lens on your camera. Did you take any pictures?"

"No."

Papà was walking along the edge of the wharf, his right hand behind his back, grasping the index and middle fingers of his left hand. I don't know if I imitated that gesture because I'd seen him do it when I was small, or whether it was a spontaneous impulse of my own body, but my way of walking—length of stride, fingers grasped, chest thrust out—was an exact replica of his own.

"Why didn't you take any pictures?"

"Robert Capa was right when he said, in the case in question, that photography never turns out well if the photographer wasn't close to the event. And I was far away from the landing."

Incidentally, the way we walk is identical to the way grandfather Rosario walked. Three different generations, the same identical gait.

"So, you wanted to get closer?"

"It's also a matter of respect, how do you know that you aren't committing an act of violence by snapping a

photograph of a human being in that exact context? Those
are situations you have to evaluate when you're in them. And
that's not all. Let's take some classic photographs as exam-
ples: *Death of a Loyalist Militiaman*, from 1936, or that little
girl hit by napalm during the Vietnam War, or the picture
of the little Syrian boy dead on the beach. How can you
help but be drawn in emotionally by these photos? But then
you catch yourself thinking: So, what have we learned from
all this? What good did any of it do, if the heartbreak just
keeps taking place? Photography puts you face-to-face with
reality—the naked little girl who's screaming and sobbing,
the dying militiaman, the drowned little Syrian boy, one of
the most horrible photographs of them all, and it's only
right that that picture was taken and then published—it
depicts a state of affairs that's agonizing, heartrending. In
spite of all this suffering displayed, though, we remain incapable of understanding what's going on. In the end, what
does any of it change?"

My father was staring at the horizon. The sea, kicked
up by the wind, looked like a battlefield after a bloodbath.
He started talking again. He hadn't completed his thought.

"Witnessing the landing, even if from a distance, was
interesting...no, 'interesting' isn't strong enough. It was a
powerful experience, but one that I lived from without, from
a remove, I was physically distant from the wharf. When
you see such a large number of people so weighed down with
suffering, the most that you can bring yourself to say is: 'It
certainly can't have been easy, it must have been terrible for

them!' Perhaps, what you ought to do is try to find a comparable situation to the desperation of people landing on an island, so that you could get closer to an understanding of what happens there, if there could ever be anything comparable that could help someone to understand that sense of bewilderment that I detected in them. For example, I think about what Uncle Beppe must be going through now, with the appearance of a lymphoma, after we had already defeated a cancer years ago . . . I don't know if I make myself clear . . . I'm talking about those situations where you feel like shouting: 'What am I supposed to do now?' and there is no answer forthcoming."

My father had made reference to his brother.

He'd mentioned his disease.

We stood there in silence staring out at the sea. The wind was covering up our breathing. The patrol boats of the Italian Coast Guard, having completed their operations, had just vanished over the horizon.

Paola, bundled in her cream-colored jacket, was talking to Alberto, the Solidarity Forum volunteer. After listening to what she had to say, the young Roman with the dreadlocks came straight toward me.

"Paola told me that you're gathering material about the things that are happening on the island. Would you be interested in meeting a diver?"

"Certainly."

Alberto pulled out his phone, dialed a number, spoke briefly, then ended the call.

"At my house, at five this afternoon. Just the two of you, he doesn't even want me to be there."

I thanked him, he explained where he lived, we exchanged phone numbers, and we said goodbye.

We got into Paola's car with her; first she had to stop by the fish vendor—"What do you have today?" "Fabulous tuna, it's still alive," *"Amunì, dammìllo"*—"All right, let me have that," she said in Sicilian, then took us to the Poliambulatorio.

"Over the years, Doctor Bartolo has been present at lots of landings, nearly all of them," Paola said. He, too, had appeared on the wharf at a certain point, during the landing operations. We met him in his office.

"These things have been happening for twenty years, do we really always have to assume that someone's going to die?"

Bartolo had begun like that, without the slightest preamble. He put on a pair of eyeglasses that had been riding on his forehead until then. My grandfather Rosario also used to wear his glasses like that when he was working on the rebuses of *La Settimana Enigmistica*, the weekly puzzle magazine. He'd hold the page very close to his face while holding his eyeglasses up on his forehead, and he'd lower them once he was ready to write in a possible solution in pencil. Only then would my grandfather hold the magazine away, so that he could contemplate the outcome of that duel of wits.

After tossing out his question, Bartolo, too, lowered his eyeglasses over his eyes and studied us for a very short time. We were his rebus. Then he raised his glasses again and went on talking: "People know things and then they pretend that they don't. That's why I'm here talking to you now, because every individual voice can help to sensitize people. We are single drops, but lots of drops can create an ocean."

He lowered his eyeglasses to the bridge of his nose again and stared at us.

"Write about it, go around and tell everything you've seen, because that's needful. On the Continent they don't have a clear idea of what's really happening down here, but I don't mean what's happening here on Lampedusa, this island is simply a point of transition, one leg of a vaster odyssey; rather I'm referring to what is really happening to these poor devils who arrive here, the atrocities they're forced to undergo, the mortification of their very existence, the demeaning of their hopes and dreams."

Pietro Bartolo is a gynecologist, he ought to be looking after life, births, new mothers, but instead he's probably the doctor who's done more inspections and identifications of corpses than any other on earth, at least outside of war zones.

"How many have I done? Too many."

It's always heartbreaking when it's a woman.

"The things they do to women, they wouldn't even dream of doing to animals," was all the doctor managed to say.

It's always worse for a woman.

The rapes are constant and repeated, both from individual rapists and gangs of them.

There are little girls who arrive here pregnant.

There are women who are transformed into toys, used roughly until they break.

Then the doctor talked about the shipwreck of October 3, 2013, the watershed event.

It was the first time I'd heard an eyewitness account of the tragedy.

Bartolo explained that, because of the vast number of corpses collected at sea, they had used the hangar at the old airport to house the dead.

There were black body bags everywhere.

"Please, God," he prayed that day, "don't let the first body bag I open have a little child inside. Please, Lord, I beg of You, not a *picciriddo*."

He screwed up his nerve, took a deep breath, and opened the bag.

"It was a *picciriddo* after all."

Pietro Bartolo experienced once again the horror of that terrible day. His hands instinctively flew up to his mouth again, as if trying to clap it shut in order to stifle a scream.

"It was just a little thing, no bigger than this. *Una co-suzza così.*"

He was measuring, once again, there in his office, the size of the child. He was pointing it out to himself more than to us. The *picciriddo* continued to appear before him every single time he thought about it, every single time he talked about it. The doctor's hands were firm as he indicated its height. No more than three feet tall. The child might have been two years old.

The doctor told us how he'd taken that little corpse in his arms, hoping it was a mistake, maybe it was still alive, he hoped it might still just be breathing, still the faintest flicker of a heartbeat, a vein pulsating, a flutter of life he could perceive by leaning in close to its nose. But no. Nothing. It was dead. The child really was dead.

That was the first corpse examined from the tragedy of October 3.

"How can we let such a small thing die? *Una creatura accussì nica?*" He dropped briefly into dialect. "I mean, we can put people on the moon, and we let human beings just die like this? There's nothing we can do to go out and get them and bring them in? Are they or are they not human beings? How long is this shame going to continue? How can we let *una cosuzza accussì nica* just die in the middle of the sea?"

A medical examiner, summoned to investigate some of the corpses retrieved from the sea and to identify them, had explained to me that there were forms upon forms to be filled out, in order to certify that this human being—with the following identifying features, with or without tattoos, with or without distinctive marks, with or without signs of abuse—was in fact now lifeless.

"In compiling the certificates, you need to be as precise as possible in your responses, so that the vested authorities have clear indications of the cause of death."

Hypothermia.

Malnutrition.

Dehydration.

Gunshot injuries.

Battery.

The body is a diary on which you can read everything that happened to it in its last days of life. The rigidity of certain muscles tells of a forced deprivation of water. The presence of very little flesh clinging to the ribcage testifies to a restricted diet over the course of long periods of time. In the lesions inflicted, there are the signs of unspeakable violence, suffered either before setting sail, in the Libyan prisons, or else aboard the refugee boat itself, because there are times when, during the crossing, the smugglers club people to death in front of all the others as a warning that it does no good to ask for water, it does no good to protest, on penalty of immediate death by clubbing and beating. Those who are killed aboard a refugee boat are usually tossed into the sea. Sometimes, those who dare to complain about the conditions they're traveling under are simply tossed into the waves, still alive.

"It's always particularly difficult to work on corpses picked up at sea," the medical examiner told me.

"The corpses are soaked in salt water, they seem like sponges," she went on. "They're all deformed: faces, muscles, internal organs. The flesh comes off, if it hasn't vanished entirely, and at times you can find the marks of fish bites. The whole body is slick and gelatinous. To the touch, it hardly even seems like a human being."

What troubled her more than anything else had taken place during the inspection of two corpses.

"Two young women, less than twenty years old, as we determined during the inspection, really very young. They were both wearing two of everything: two sweatshirts, two shirts, two pairs of jeans, two pairs of panties, one over the other. It was as if they had put on everything they owned, clothing and the clothing they'd change into, to ward off the cold, no doubt, but also so that they could take everything with them. In an internal pocket, they'd stitched in sheets of paper with addresses. That was their treasure, the contacts to call in Europe. They'd chased after the hope of a more dignified life, wearing double clothing as a protection and as a memory. Then, once we'd stripped them naked, we began our inspection."

They had died during the trip across, from hypothermia.

They both bore the marks of repeated rapes.

Outside of the Poliambulatorio, it was nice in the bright sun; it was no longer necessary to wear a jacket. We got into the car. The cockpit had a faint aroma of fresh-caught tuna.

Paola started talking.

"Since we're outsiders on Lampedusa, it's easier for me and for Melo to establish relationships with other outsiders, rather than with the Lampedusans. They're mistrustful, the Lampedusans. If you weren't born here, as far as they're concerned you'll never understand a thing, about the island and about life in general. That means it's easier for us to become close with, to establish human ties with anyone who shares your condition: that of being the guest of a place where you weren't born. In particular, almost immediately, we made friends with the young people who worked in the welcome center on behalf of such organizations as the Red Cross, the UNHCR, and Save the Children. We just happened to meet, I don't even remember how. In that same group there was a friend who was a radiologist."

Paola drove slowly, without haste. She wanted to get through that memory during the drive, so that she could leave it in the car, and not bring it with her into her home. She had created a situation of something close to silence, the car was rolling along, and the asphalt rattled and crumbled beneath the wheels with the sound of crunching gravel.

Suddenly my father spoke up.

"If he was a radiologist, he ought to have done a round of X-rays to establish whether the youngsters were legally of age."

Paola nodded.

I hadn't understood the reasoning behind that observation and Papà explained to me that the length of the bones is one of the data points for establishing a person's age, along with the presence or absence of pubic hair on the genitalia.

"Yes, that was one of my friend's tasks," Paola confirmed. "Minors are treated under one rubric, legal adults another," was the last thing she had to say on the subject, after which she parked in front of the bakery, got out with the engine still running, hurried in to get the bread she'd ordered, and then climbed back in behind the wheel.

"Often, we'd eat dinner with the other off-islanders. Their accounts were fundamental in helping me understand what was going on. It was thanks to them that I was able to get closer to this situation. In particular, I remember the stories that had to do with the conditions of the women who arrived on Lampedusa. A friend of ours, a gynecologist, told me that one afternoon she examined, right here, a woman who'd been genitally circumcised, and that had shocked her deeply. Sure, she'd studied infibulation, but she'd never actually laid eyes on such a thing in real life. That was the only time anything so deeply upset her, and we're talking about a professional with more than thirty years of solid experience behind her. I remember all those stories with extreme clarity. The rapes suffered in Libya. The incredibly high percentage of rapes. The suspicion that the great number of pregnant women who arrive on Lampedusa is bound up with the fact that, precisely because they're pregnant, they can no longer be used. The explanation of the burns that so many of the women have suffered. Here's what happens: In the rubber dinghies, the women are put in the center, seated. They don't sit on the inflated tubes of the sides. And on the floor of those rubber dinghies a devastating mixture often accumulates—sea water, gasoline, and urine—highly blistering. And so the women suffer from serious blistering, in very delicate parts of the body. Blistering of the women's genitalia is a grim constant of landing sites. The women in those stories were all very young. I don't believe that any of them, and I mean not a single one, in spite of being through medical briefings, chose to have an abortion."

Paola parked. Outside the car window, the sea, whipped by the sirocco wind, was blue and clear. If it had been hotter out, we would have dived right in, Papà and I, and we would have taken a swim, slow, steady strokes, out to the end of the cape enclosing the cove, the sea like an embrace, immersed in the water like a baptism, the swim as a way of getting the burden of the day off our backs.

Papà decided to go take a nap.

"In the afternoon, I'll take a walk around the town, maybe I'll have a chance to take a few photographs."

"You're not eating lunch?"

"I'm not very hungry."

"Neither am I, maybe later we can get together for dinner."

I wandered around Lampedusa. Everything was deserted. A ghost town. I felt like I was in a western. Along the main street, I saw only stray mutts, stretched out, slumbering.

I called Silvia; that emptiness was making me anxious, and only my girlfriend could help me tough it out.

"Ciao."

"My love, how are you?"

"You know what? The perception is that here in town basically none of what happens at sea filters through. Everything is restricted to the wharf or else inside the Center. And yet, seeing that the town is basically deserted, the only people who seem to live in Lampedusa are those wearing a uniform."

"Yes, okay, but how are you?" Silvia asked again.

All the shutters on the windows were fastened tight. There were no shops open, and the sirocco alone dominated the scene.

But it was my inner landscape that interested her.

"I feel all hollowed out."

At the other end of the line, I heard her breathe, then slowly smile.

"Don't identify with the town. You're not a deserted town, you're just someone walking through a deserted town, if anything."

I had been pierced by all that emptiness.

"How are the cats?" I asked her.

Silvia laughed.

"Now, that's a sensible question. They're fine, Pepa is the same princess as always, and Soba veers between moments of sweetness and sheer madness. How are you?"

"Now that I'm talking to you, I'm already feeling better."

"There, that's the spirit. How is it going with your papà?"

"Fine. Right now I think he's taking a nap, but I'm going to go on walking through the town. Soon I'll start talking to people again."

"Well, I hope your work goes well, then."

I'd walked the pedestrian mall in one direction, and I phoned Uncle Beppe while walking it in the other direction, with the sea straight ahead of me as a vanishing point.

"Beppuzzo, how are you?"

"Daviduzzo! Today I feel a little tired, but yesterday I worked out with weights. I'm going to beat that damned tumor. How's it going on Lampedusa?"

"*È un chiummo ma anche una piuma.*" It's as heavy as a lump of lead, but also light as a feather.

"Then hurry up and finish writing this book, I'm eager to read it. Is Francesco with you?"

"No, not now, God only knows where Papà is, I think at the bed and breakfast. I'm out walking around alone. In fact, he's perfectly capable of calling you now, and it would be one to zero for you, Uncle."

"I hope he does."

"What are you going to do now? Read a book?"

"No, no, I'm going to go take me a nap. You want to talk later on?"

"Certainly, Uncle, enjoy your nap. I'll call you tonight before dinner, kisses to you."

In town, the only sound was the gusting of the wind. It pushed, then it would subside for a moment, fooling you into thinking it had stopped, and then it started beating against the houses and rocks again.

I ran my forefinger down the page of the phone book. I found the number of the Roman volunteer, Alberto, whom I still hadn't called. I felt so alone that I called him, even though it was more than an hour till my appointment with the diver at his house.

He answered immediately.

"I'm going out to buy some fish. You want to go with? I'll swing by and pick you up in my car."

Alberto had been living on Lampedusa for many months now. He was under thirty and he had a Roman accent, detectable but not overwhelming. The long dreadlocks that were so striking hung down well below his shoulder blades.

"Have you ever had any problems on account of your hair?" I asked, pointing at it.

"Not here in town, no. On the wharf, once, even though I like to remember a fine moment I experienced thanks to my dreadlocks."

A young Senegalese man had landed, and he, too, had dreadlocks. When he came face to face with Alberto who was giving him hot tea, he hugged Alberto and called him "Brother." They talked about reggae and the beatings the young man had been given in Libya before he managed to get aboard a refugee boat.

At every intersection, even though we had the right of way, Alberto came to a full stop, the best approach to follow in a place where the rules of the traffic code were considered guidelines more than actual laws.

"But when was the time that your dreadlocks caused you problems?"

"A new police official had come to the island. The police force is in charge of the kids once they set foot on dry land. That functionary caused us lots of problems, for us volunteers but for others as well, and even went so far as to evict us from the wharf for several weeks. And about me, in particular, he said that I was a fucking long-haired freak."

"And then?"

"And then, once his stretch on the island came to an end, he was sent somewhere else."

We parked in front of the fish store.

"There's this one kind of fish you can only find here, the bluefish. It's incredible, it lives on the lower seabeds, it's just exquisite grilled."

His eyes were dancing happily as he told me.

The fishmonger was gutting and cleaning the fish. The mullets on the display counter were beautiful, and I asked Alberto how he had come to be on Lampedusa. He told me that he had studied anthropology in Rome, management and planning of social services in London, he'd interned for six months with the United Nations in Turin, and then, after receiving a job offer to work in the field, he had moved to Lampedusa.

When the fish was ready, Alberto paid and we got in the car.

"We're really early," he said. It was forty-five minutes till my appointment. He turned on the engine and started talking again.

"Was this your first landing?" he asked.

"Yes."

"And the first for your father, too, I imagine."

"Yes."

"So, what do you think?"

"It was an experience.... I don't know what adjective to use: Heartbreaking? Overwhelming? Powerful? A combination of the three, maybe."

"That's the way it was for me, too, the very first landing I witnessed was a hallucinatory experience. My hands were sweating. I was very, very, very tense: That arrival was sheer madness, it's one hundred fifty miles from Libya to Lampedusa! The idea that human beings would have set out on such a journey aboard a flimsy rubber dinghy struck me as truly absurd! That they could have set out with little water, little food, children aboard, after living months and months in industrial sheds in Libya, with no idea of whether they'd die on the open seas, well: All of these considerations, amplified by the fact that I was, so to speak, touching this reality with my own hands for the very first time, just overwhelmed me."

He stared at the road ahead of him the whole time he spoke, driving slowly.

"It took place at night. I can clearly remember the yellow lights reflecting off the thermal blankets. Those gleams were beautiful, they seemed like stars emerging from the darkness. I was especially struck by the natural way that the people around me were dealing with that event. 'Wait, they're willing to joke about this?' I remember thinking. Facing us was the unknown, we had no idea who was going to be coming, whether there would be dead people, what was going to happen. The wharf seemed to me like a...well I won't say a sacred place, but still a place where you might be expected to maintain a certain level of comportment, where a person ought to behave respectfully. But that's just the way the mind works: It normalizes things, otherwise we'd all go insane. If I were to reflect seriously and continually about the brutality of the border, about the things that the people I saw landing have experienced, quite simply I'd be unable to go on living. I'd live badly, in any case. What's more, it starts to become routine. How many landings have I witnessed? Two hundred? If you do something two hundred times, sooner or later you're going to get used to it. What's more, the need to get used to it and, as a result, behave in a professional fashion when these young people arrive, also derives from the need to show that we are reliable individuals. The situation on the wharf is always delicate and, like I told you, there are forces at play that would just as soon get rid of us."

He parked, turned off the engine, took the key out of the ignition, but remained seated. He was a calm young man in everything he did: rolling up the window, putting the car in reverse, smiling.

"But I'd like to make it clear that, normally, the situations we experience at the wharf are by no means tragic, aside from those three, four, five times that the situation really did become dire. All the other times, it was really a party."

"For real?"

"I've seen people dance and kiss the ground the minute they disembark, I've seen others pray, the way Muslims do, stretched out with their forehead pressed down, and others clap and stamp out a rhythm with their hands and feet. I have beautiful memories. More than once, it happened that the young men arrived in the port applauding and singing, even while they were still aboard the patrol boat. It's really a stupendous apparition to witness a patrol boat at night, coming in so festively from the darkness of the sea. Maybe I'm overstepping my bounds here, but I believe that the experience of the wharf is one of the happiest interludes in the lives of these young people, in part because the experiences they're going to have just a short while later are going to be very, very different. But after all the things they've been through, after the crossing, here at last is dry land. There on the wharf is a new birth, full of hope and joy. And you find yourself in the role of the first person to welcome them. They've faced horrible situations, they deserve a welcome worthy of the name. As far as I'm concerned, it's a privilege to be there, because you honor their journey, their courage, and even their recklessness, by taking part for even a brief instant in their journey."

Alberto wasn't getting out of the car.

He was still stalling.

A shiver whipped my back, my intuition had lit up: Was this an octopus moment?

I was at the beach at Scopello with my uncle Beppe, I might have been seven years old, and I'd gotten it into my head that I needed to learn to catch an octopus. My father wasn't on vacation yet and was working at the hospital. My mother was on holiday, but she'd remained at home with my little brother, and in any case, she wasn't cut out for octopus hunting, so it was my uncle who got caught up in it.

"Come on, I'll take Daviduzzo down to the sea."

"To catch an octopus, Uncle."

"Certainly."

I was gripping a sharpened pole and the water came up to my chest. Uncle Beppe was standing next to me. With the gentle demeanor that he's always had, he was explaining to me how you catch an octopus. He was on edge but he was doing his best not to let it show. He was speaking in little more than a whisper.

"In order to get the octopus out of its den, you have to remain motionless, with your pole ready to strike. Don't move. The octopus will come to you. If you move toward it and you force the moment, the octopus will flee, and you'll never catch it."

I don't know where on earth he got all that information. Maybe he had a past as an octopus hunter and this was just the first time he'd ever told anyone about it. We remained motionless for a very long time. When the muscles in my arms started to shake and I wanted to drop the harpoon and swim back to shore, because boredom had swallowed my mind and even my soul, at that moment, when I was about to give up any ambitions to hunt anything, behold the octopus. It looked like a moving stain. It was swimming along slowly. Its tentacles tugged into its body with disorderly laziness. There was nothing else but the sea, me, the octopus, and Uncle Beppe. As predicted, the octopus came straight up to me. Uncle Beppe was chewing his lip and holding his breath, even though his immobility transmitted anxiety and discomfort. But I was far too focused on becoming a great and respected octopus hunter. This was going to be the exploit of the summer. I strengthened my grip on the harpoon, took a deep breath and, when the time came to release the harpoon, my arm didn't move. I just stood there, harpoon in hand, and eyes fixed on the octopus which, blithely unaware, swam away out into the open water.

Uncle Beppe heaved a sigh of relief.

"Oh well, it was little," I said, as if to excuse myself.

"You were right, and not just right, but absolutely right, not to stab him," Uncle Beppe replied.

He was all relaxed and smiling now.

We got out of the water.

"Uncle, but how did you know how to catch an octopus?"

"Someone taught me," Beppe replied, running his hand through the hair, now thinning, on his head. Then he pulled out a beach towel and started drying my hair.

"Who taught you?" I insisted.

"Your father."

Once we were dry, we went back indoors.

An octopus moment is when a story, if it chooses to, comes toward you, there's no need to stab it or lunge in its direction. It's necessary to stay close to it, that much is true, you must respect its timing and be ready to welcome it with every fiber of your being. That's all.

Alberto had released his grip on the steering wheel. He'd relaxed his shoulders into the backrest, loosening his arms, letting his eyelids half-close, rubbing the back of his neck. After a long breath, he opened his eyes again. He was ready to talk.

"It still upsets me to remember a landing that took place one night in late August. We had gone down to the wharf as usual, feeling relatively carefree. We were joking around and laughing. Of the roughly two hundred twenty people who disembarked, the first ones to walk down onto the wharf were in pretty good shape, but they were the only ones who were in good shape. None of us could even begin to imagine what was about to happen in just a few short minutes. An apocalypse here on earth. As if an airplane had crashed and we were the first responders. Everyone else, about two hundred people, still aboard the patrol boat, wasn't even in good enough shape to walk. They were crying. They had burns and blisters all over their bodies. The first of these to be taken off the boat were carried and loaded onto gurneys and into ambulances. But after that, on an island that possesses just three ambulances, and on a wharf where there were no more than four, maybe five gurneys, there were still a hundred eighty people in need of medical attention. And every one of them, one way or another, had medical problems, ranging from the very grave to the less urgent, where the least urgent problem—I remember all too clearly—consisted of those who were weeping without stopping, as they shouted: 'I've lost my brother,' 'I've lost my wife,' 'I've lost my friend.' They had watched as the refugee boat next to them sank under the waves."

Alberto's phrases had drawn out, dilated. When he wasn't talking, his hands went up to cover his face, as if trying to hold onto something that was no longer there, a face, a pair of shoulders, a hand.

"I was face-to-face with a sobbing woman. She was shouting: 'I've lost my son, I lost my son in the deep blue sea.' And she was telling me. Me, as I was standing face-to-face with her. What could I ever say to her? How could I ever help her? I couldn't seem to speak, I couldn't seem to do absolutely anything."

The silence had penetrated into his story. It had taken its own space.

"Some of us burst into tears. It was a complete collapse of the established order. Given the enormous number of the wounded, we all participated in the landing operations, not just those who were assigned to that responsibility. We'd take people as they came off the boat and lay them down right on the wharf. One young woman passed out in my arms. That's right, all the fainting. People passed out constantly. And those with burns were really and truly grave."

He scrabbled with his fingers in his bag of tobacco. He rolled himself a cigarette and put it in the center of the bag.

"Once the landing was over, before going home I went down to the beach at Cala Pisana. I went for a swim and I felt better. I often use the sea to assuage my anxiety. Water as a form of purification. It seems metaphorical, but it really works. No one else was there. It was dawn."

For a few minutes already, every time he paused, Alberto had started to chew on the inside of his cheek. Just then, his teeth hadn't yet released their grip. The octopus moment was not yet over.

"One last memory. A week after that horrible landing there were twenty-five, maybe thirty deaths at sea. But the landing at the wharf, incredibly, went smoothly. The people who reached dry land weren't upset, they had no injuries, they weren't in a state of shock. They were all just happy to be there. They unloaded a dead young man, who was just left lying on the wharfside from the very beginning of operations—he was the first to be disembarked onto dry land—and no one bothered to cover him with a sheet. It's the kind of thing you see all the time in the movies: There's a dead person, you cover them up with a sheet. There was nothing we could do about it, and, to tell the truth, it was not something that I wanted or want to do. It doesn't take much to cover a dead person with a sheet, why should I have to go do it when there are people sent there specifically to do that job, among other things? That young man is buried in the cemetery now. His name is Yassin. But there's still no name on his grave. If it hadn't been for the fact that we gathered information about him right at the time of the landing, we would never have known anything about his name and his story. Yassin had a wife and daughter in Sweden, legal residents, so he could have made an application to be reunited with his family, but instead he died at sea. That's something worth thinking about: If these truly were humanitarian missions, when someone dies we might bother to collect information from the survivors so that we can at least reconstruct the names of the deceased. But no one does that. Instead, investigations are undertaken immediately to determine the name of the person running the vessel, where they set sail. There is a very specific desire for actionable intelligence, and none at all for the more distinctly humanitarian aspect. So now there's nothing on that young man's grave, just a smear of cement and nothing more."

Alberto opened the bag of tobacco again, pulled out the freshly rolled cigarette, and raised it to his mouth.

"And now, let's go in."

The house was spartan and bare, like every house in vacation spots: at the center of the room, a table with four wicker chairs, on the wall, a couple of bookshelves, a very old TV set without a remote sitting on a small white cabinet, a little refrigerator, practically no plates or utensils in the dish rack.

There was a knock at the door.

Alberto went to answer it.

The diver walked into the room.

"No tape recorders," were his first words.

He was enormous.

I WAS NEXT to the Testa di Polpo rocks.

Papà had joined me.

Sunset had just begun.

"How did your interview with the diver go?"

My father's blue eyes were still, quiet, and welcoming.

Here's what I felt like telling him: It was an encounter that shook me deeply, Papà, because of its implications concerning life and death, because of the unsolvable dilemmas that emerged, because of the enormous depth of post-traumatic stress that I sensed in him. Coming face-to-face with someone directly involved in these matters called everything into question—my preconceptions, the categories I use, even the way I think. Just for starters, I really had no idea of what actually happens out there.

And I'd have gone on like this: Definitions mean nothing, they're incapable of rendering the complexity of an event or of a human being. Perhaps, in the end, it all comes down to a simple fork in the road: If there's a person drowning in a stormy sea, who am I? The one who dives in, even if it means risking my life, or the one who, terrified of death, remains safely clinging to dry land?

That's what I would have liked to tell him.

My father was standing there, facing me, ready to take in any consideration I might venture, anything I felt compelled to vent.

There was no judgment in his light blue eyes.

I dropped my gaze.

"It went well, Papà. It went well."

If we hadn't talked in such a long time, the blame wasn't all his.

It takes two to create a dialogue.

I'd been missing from that construction myself.

And he'd missed me.

"What did you do this afternoon?" I asked him, to escape from the silence between the two of us that had now become intolerable to me.

Papà started by describing to me the route he'd followed from Cala Pisana to the Porto Vecchio, or Old Port, by way of the town.

"The place is full of stray dogs," he observed.

"I took some pictures of them," he went on.

"I've always wanted a dog," was the conclusion of the warp and weave of his thoughts.

Papà held the display of the digital camera closer to his face, and then he showed me the pictures. There were shots full of dogs. Lying under marble benches, those stray mutts were the only life-form in that autumn in a town that was otherwise completely spectral. Their eyes were closed, their bodies sprawled on the ground. There was a great deal of depth in his pictures, with the sea in the background as the omnipresent vanishing point. Then, I saw one of the pictures I was expecting. It was a detail of a dog's eye. Papà had gotten very close to the stray mutt to get a shot of its open pupil. At the center of the pupil was him, kneeling, with his camera in front of his face, caught at the instant that the shutter snapped. In the next photo, the dog's pupil was turned toward the bottom corner, where I could see Papà's arm. He was petting the dog with that hand, prompting a mixed reaction of surprise and gratitude.

"Papà, weren't you afraid of the dogs?"

"No, they were good dogs."

I felt like resting my head on his chest, but I didn't.

Papà showed me the next pictures: details of broken walls, tufts of weeds sprouting from the sidewalk, the triumphant rust on the skeleton of a bicycle left to wither for too many summers.

Then, right afterward, like a slap in the face, a new sequence of photographs.

I couldn't believe it.

At the center of these snapshots was me. It was me, photographed from behind. There I was, slouching along down Via Roma, talking on the phone with Silvia and with Uncle Beppe, jotting down a few thoughts, holding my head in my hands.

My father had taken my picture without telling me.

I hadn't noticed a thing.

It had always been this way. In a very real sense, Papà had never stopped watching my back. Like when I'd learned to ride a bicycle. I would pedal through the streets of Palermo, and he'd follow me in his car, a good hundred and fifty feet back. That's one of the happiest memories of my life. In my memory, there were just the three of us: me, him, and our Palermo.

Was this what it meant to you to be my father? Following me in silence as I walk through thorns and rubble, without losing track of me?

If I'd never noticed his presence, it had been because in our relationship I placed more importance on the things that were missing, the words, rather than weighing the one thing that had always been there, the gaze.

If he hadn't intervened, it was because at a certain point, I had kept him from helping me.

"Papà, why did you become a doctor?" I asked him, turning back to stare into his blue eyes, in an attempt at dialogue that I immediately judged to be pathetic.

Sometimes we build walls without even realizing it.

It really had been a long day.

Instead, Papà started simultaneously smiling and blushing.

"Why did I become a doctor?"

He was all red in the face, but he went on looking at me.

"Yes."

What with the blue of his irises and the red of his blazing cheeks, he really did look like a young boy.

"To escape from what I really would have liked to become instead: a writer."

The smile persisted on his face, like a liberation.

The water continued to crash against the rocks. Cala Pisana was completely illuminated by the sunset, Paola had just stuck her head out the window, telling us that dinner was ready, Papà had already turned to go, and I was still standing there, in the vortex of the sirocco, defenseless, heartbroken, riven by the fall of night.

I often called Uncle Beppe to talk to him about something that had struck me.

It was easy to talk with him.

"You know the archipelago of the Pelagian Islands? It's made up of three islands."

"Lampedusa, Linosa, and..."

"Lampione, a small desert island. The name of the archipelago comes directly from the Greek πέλαγος, which, and I quote verbatim, 'indicates the sea that, in constant movement, incessantly torments the shores with its waves.' Did you know that this tiny archipelago represents the meeting point of two continents, Africa and Europe?"

"No."

"Neither did I."

I had studied the geology of Lampedusa a little, and I had learned some things that intrigued me. I doled out the information that I'd jotted down, parsimoniously, trying to build up to a crescendo.

"Linosa is Europe, it's volcanic in origin, in fact it's covered with craters. Lampedusa, on the other hand, isn't of volcanic origin because it belongs to the African tectonic plate."

"It's part of Africa?" my uncle asked with sincere astonishment.

He, too, was impressed by this information.

We really were uncle and nephew.

"Yes. Technically it's an elevated sector of the African tectonic plate."

"A highland jutting out of the water," my uncle mused. "How nice," he went on. "The southernmost island in all of Europe and the African continent are the same piece of land."

It was a cultural naval battle.

What was shelled and sunk were our certainties.

"According to the scientific model of plate tectonics, it's as if the earth were split up into different pieces of a big jigsaw puzzle. Each of those puzzle pieces represents a section of the tectonic plate. These puzzle pieces are set down next to each other and they move, moving apart, moving back together, hitting each other."

"It's as if the earth were alive," said Beppe.

"Exactly. What's more, I saw a bathymetric map of the Mediterranean Sea, which showed the measurements of the depths of the sea. In the section of sea between Lampedusa and Africa, the seabed is shallow, a hundred feet for the most part, sometimes as deep as a hundred fifty feet. To the north, on the other hand, as you move toward Europe, the seabed drops sharply, sinking immediately to thirteen hundred feet, and after that deeper, to thirty-two hundred feet and even more. There's practically a canyon between the two continents, but it's disappearing because, as you know, they're coming unarrestably closer: Africa and Eurasia are involved in a process of compression. The two continents are crashing."

The old structures were falling, prejudices were collapsing.

At the other end of the line, I could hear my uncle breathing louder.

"When two plates meet, one will slide under the other, diving down to the earth's mantle. Guess which of the two plates is undergoing subduction? The Eurasian plate. Eurasia, inevitably, is going to be pushed under Africa."

My uncle emitted a sound that was midway between a smile and a dawning realization. A shifting of plates that lasts for millions of years. Entire eras to make a separation official, entire eras to stitch it back together. The Planet's use of time is not as limited as a human being's use of time. Inevitability operates over the long term.

"Well, anyway, I just wanted to share these thoughts with you."

"Why?" my uncle asked me.

"Because what's happening now in the Mediterranean can be seen as a simple preview of the future: That which was separated is being rejoined. The movement, the shifting, the migration all belong to the very life of the Planet. Birds migrate, fish migrate, the seas move, and flocks and continents shift from here to there. It's going to happen. It's happening now. Africa is going to arrive and it's going to perch on top of Europe, or what's left of Europe."

"Like a sheet," said Beppuzzo.

"Or a shroud," was my comment.

We said goodbye.

"Daviduzzo, I'm really tired, forgive me."

I hadn't thought that just talking on the phone could exhaust him to this point.

"Don't worry, Uncle. Have a good rest."

Were these the effects of the chemo?

When we ended the phone call, I stood there for a while with the phone in my hand, uncertain. There was something that didn't add up. Then, all of a sudden, I realized that Uncle hadn't asked me why I was so struck by the collision between continents, but rather why I'd felt the need to share that particular piece of information with him of all people.

I sat there a little while longer, wondering whether Uncle Beppe asked my father those same questions.

———

I'D HEARD THE NAME of Lampedusa for the first time when I was a *picciriddo*. For a number of months my mother had gone there on behalf of the hospital, to work with children who displayed serious learning disabilities. When she left, Papà would take me and my brother—back then we were the only two of the four children we'd eventually become—to lunch and dinner at the restaurant across the street, and we'd spend every afternoon at the movie theater watching science fiction movies. In that period, I developed the concept of "island of an island." We were Sicily, and Lampedusa, even though it maintained the peculiarities typical of any island—the solitude that came with the fact that it was surrounded by the sea,—was a fragment of Sicily, a distant satellite that orbits the mother ship, just like the Aeolian Islands, or the Aegadian Islands, or the stacks and sea cliffs of Scopello. Island of an island. My mother later confirmed that it was true: On Lampedusa they spoke our same language, they ate our same food, they used our same swear words. Upon her return from her trips, she'd continually sing the praises of the island's harsh beauty.

"There's not a tree for love or money, and it's dark, dark, dark."

She often luxuriated in her descriptions of the sea.

"It's deeply moving."

In her words you could detect the platonic ideal of transparency.

Thirty-plus years later, when Lampedusa had become a symbol in the global imagination, my mother recovered a tile in her memory from that period of working there.

"There was this one kid, out of all the others, who made a profound impression on me. He had a sharp gaze, and he was a real hoodlum when it came to studying. *'A che mi sèrbi studiàri?'* he'd always answer back with contempt, motionless in front of the blank page and the sharpened pencil. 'What good does it do me to study?' He wasn't interested in the slightest in learning to read and write, and in fact he refused to even take it in his hand, the pencil. That child wanted only one thing, to go fishing with his father and his grandfather."

She had gone to visit him at home and there she had discovered that he played the guitar exceedingly well. His uncle had taught him how. My mother, after long meetings with the principal and the other teachers at the school, convinced the entire teaching staff and that child to come to this compromise: The *picciriddo* would give his fellow students guitar lessons, teaching them chords and notes, and in exchange he'd try to learn to write. A tit for tat: He knew how to play, the others knew how to write, and it's only right for friends to teach each other things.

In the afternoons they spent together, that boy had told my mother about the mornings he'd spent clinging to the shoals, trying to catch a crab barehanded, confiding to her the thoughts that had passed through his head while waiting for that crustacean. The horizon, for example, was to his mind a line of earth and sand, and therefore, to the north of

Lampedusa, that line was Sicily and to the south it was all
of Africa. Then he told her that in the future he planned to
own a boat, and that he would christen it *Cernia*, or 'Grou-
per,' like the queen of fish, and he'd go out fishing every
blessed day, except on weekends—weekends are when you
stay home with your family, your wife and your children.
And while he was out on his fishing expeditions, at noon,
when the fish are careful because they can see the nets, well,
that's when he'd go back to dry land to get a nap, because
dreams you have on the sea get lost in the night, and he'd
lie down for his nap on a beach somewhere, sometimes in
Sicily, other times in Africa, depending on the wind and the
currents, and before falling asleep, he'd always turn his head
to look toward his home, Lampedusa, a button in the middle of the sea that holds together two different continents.

THE FIRST TIME was in the summer of 1991. My folks
had left with my brothers for a holiday in the Dolomites, I
wanted to spend some time at the beach so I stayed behind
all alone in Palermo. One of my friends remembered that he
had a cousin on Lampedusa who had a house that he said
was cozy and so, without giving it too much thought, we
filled our backpacks with scuba masks, beach towels, and
six-packs of beer, and barely nine hours later we'd ridden
our Vespas from Palermo to Porto Empedocle. We boarded
the ferry at night and the next morning we were landing at

Lampedusa. I remember little if anything of that trip. I had the distinct impression that I was on an extension of Sicily, but it was a Sicily arrested at some point thirty years earlier, the way it must have been in my parents' day, when Mamma wore flower-print dresses and Papà wore black-rimmed eyeglasses. The house where we stayed was tiny and by no means cozy. There were seven of us sleeping on the ground, our sleeping bags all unzipped and pillows and cushions scattered across the floor. We were seventeen years old, and the musculature of our backs was still plenty elastic, the same as the musculature of our hearts: We might suffer the grief of abandonment, but then our eyes met a seductive gaze and our grief was as good as forgotten, vanished from our loins and our chests. It was blistering hot. "Fuck but where are we anyway, in Africa?" we'd say over and over, laughing every time at what we thought was a wisecrack.

When the wind kicked up, it exploded in your head.

"Jesus, what *is* that?"

"*Libeccio*, is what the fisherman said."

"Where does it come from?"

"*Libeccio*, it's from Libya."

"It's murderous."

This wasn't a wind. This was a shameless display of power. Only underwater could you escape the lashes of its tyranny.

We ate bread and olives for three days, the only food we could afford. We kept looking for a place to go dancing, but we had no luck. There were no boats to take us on a tour of the island because they were all out doing deep-sea fishing. We failed miserably at our every attempt to strike up a conversation with the opposite sex.

"What should we do, go back home? It's easier to pick up chicks in Mondello!"

"Let's go."

There hadn't been a love at first sight between me and the island. I left it without knowing when and if I'd ever come back, the hatch of the ship closed behind me and I didn't even bother to turn around, not a farewell, not an *arrivederci*, no romantic longing. I was reading the latest issue of the comic book *Dylan Dog* and I was humming "Have You Ever Been (To Electric Ladyland)" to look cool. Consumed by anxiety over my final high school exams the following summer and the terror that I might be alone for the rest of my life, all I wanted was to find a pair of red lips that could break my heart, and I yearned with every ounce of my being to write a great protest song with a vibrant electric guitar solo. That three-day stay was nothing more than a pin stuck in my mental map of Sicilian places: Lampedusa, been there, done that, next!

Palermo, in that summer of 1991, was a ferocious beast, ready to savage you for a parking space or a glance held steady too long.

Kicked to pieces, the city's nerves were shot.

Even if it was down on its knees, it slashed at anyone with its talons extended.

My mother, on the phone, kept repeating the usual mother kind of things: "The Dolomites are beautiful, everyone's dressed in Tyrolean garb, the grass looks like a lake, that's how vast the meadows are. Now, about you, be careful when you're out and about. Are you washing regularly? Are you keeping the house clean? Are you eating? Are you washing the dishes or am I going to find Dante's Inferno when we get back?"

Suddenly, a radical shift.

"Hold on, let me put your father on."

She must have caught him off guard, too, because for the first twenty seconds or so we both said nothing, listening to our reciprocal breathing.

In the end, the curtain rose on our dialogue.

"Ciao, Papà."

"Ciao."

"How is it in the Dolomites?"

"It's the mountains."

"I was on Lampedusa."

"How is it?"

"It's the sea."

"Nice, then."

"Maybe some day I'll take you there."

"Sure, maybe."

"Well then, ciao."

"Ciao."

When we didn't know what to say to each other on the phone, I'd noticed that Papà and I assumed the same physical posture: left hand in pocket, feet planted solidly on the ground, body swaying nervously forward and back, right hand busy crushing the receiver, as if imploring that receiver itself to put an end to the conversation. Our emotions transferred themselves into our bodies in the exact same manner. The same for him as it was for me: My breathing needed to turn jagged at the moment anguish invaded, a stab in the ribs, a contraction around the shoulder blades, and, immediately afterward, the explosion of a headache that simply couldn't be handled without an analgesic. We were two separate pages inked in the same handwriting. Is that what being father and son meant? The duplication of emotions in the body, and succumbing to them in the same way?

I CONTINUED TO COME BACK to Lampedusa.

Uncle Beppe had never been.

He would really have liked swimming here, I thought as I stared at Cala Pisana, vowing that someday I'd take Beppe to the island, just as I had my father.

"One day we'll come here together," I'd told him over the phone, in a boastful tone of voice.

"When I'm better," he'd replied, bringing me back to reality with just a few words.

I'D WITNESSED MORE than twenty landings.

One had lasted from midnight to 1:40 AM. I was on the highest section of the Molo Favaloro with an Italian Coast Guard officer.

He said to me: "After years, what happens to us is something similar to what happens to skin exposed too long to the sun. When it hardens, it becomes a kind of armor. But what really matters is what you have inside you. We're talking about *pietas*, about human beings, about a desperate attempt to cut the number of deaths out on the sea down to zero. A crazy battle we're fighting, a battle worthy of Don Quixote. But we still fight it every blessed day."

The patrol boat pulled over and moored, the landing operation began.

He added: "There's nothing finer than to see children arrive, alive."

Wrapped in a blanket, a *piccirìdda* not even two years old. The giant diver I'd met at Alberto's house was holding her in his arms. The little girl wasn't crying, she was calm, sleeping.

Then the girls started disembarking.

They were almost all Nigerian, and very young.

They might be anywhere from twelve to fifteen years old.
There were two hundred thirty-seven of them.

FEBRUARY HAD TURNED the whole day leaden and gray.

It was almost cold at Cala Pisana.

The evening was taking possession of the horizon.

I picked up my phone and dialed the number, while waiting for either Paola or Melo to pop their head out to tell me that dinner was ready.

"Ciao Papà."

"Hey, how are you?"

"I'm back on Lampedusa."

My position on the checkerboard of the world was the only possible response.

I'm a geography.

I have the island's state of mind.

It was all so blurry.

In order to start to get my ideas organized, I needed a trigger.

The roar of the mistral echoed in my head.

Alone, I could never have done it.

When I was a *piccirìddo*, I'd been stung by three wasps on my left shoulder blade. Mamma was holding my hand, I was biting a pillow, and Papà was extracting the stingers, using a needle and a knife.

Even in that Lampedusan winter, Papà was necessary to extract the new thorns that were tormenting me.

He asked me: "Who did you see today?"

Alone, I wasn't capable of saving myself.

And so I surrendered to the abyss, naming the first image that popped into my mind, without mediation, without elaboration, in spite of the fact that I was ashamed because it said so much more about me than I was willing to let show through.

"Papà, I met a samurai."

He was forty-four years old. A commander in the Italian Coast Guard, he had a 300 Class patrol boat. His everyday existence and the lives of his crew can easily be summarized: Go out on the sea at any hour of the day or night, in any weather, the minute a rescue call comes in. When he wasn't out on the sea, he was training with his men on dry land.

He told me: "Training helps you to face life. To put up with the fatigue. To tolerate the suffering. We train so that we torment ourselves as little as we absolutely must. Our torment is all for the people we are unable to save."

He was a bundle of nerves.

He'd been practicing this profession for twenty-six years.

"We've increased the exercises specifically for the chest and the shoulders, inserting targeted routines into our training. During the rescues, people who've fallen into the sea are no longer able to move their legs, they've remained motionless aboard the refugee boat for too many hours in the same position. They're exhausted, dehydrated, in some cases unconscious. One morning we pulled thirteen hundred people out of the water, by the strength of our arms alone, one after another, one body at a time. It went on for hours."

His skin was darkened and weathered by constant exposure to bright sunlight.

His forehead was creased by fine wrinkles, like furrows carved out by the wind.

He had the regal bearing of a noble warrior.

He's a samurai, I decided.

A samurai commanding a patrol boat in the open Mediterranean waters.

"What's his name?" Papà asked over the phone.

"Giuseppe," I replied.

"Just like your uncle," said Papà, before sinking into an emotionally significant, shamelessly narrative silence. When he called his brother "your uncle," my father was conferring upon me a role—that of nephew—in their fraternal relationship, and at the same establishing a certain distance between himself and Beppe. My father really was very worried about the tumor that had invaded Beppe's body. The only time I'd ever seen him so apprehensive was when I had just turned fourteen and I was dying from a case of bronchopneumonia with an allergic reaction. That April afternoon my temperature spiked to well over 106 degrees. I was delirious. I could no longer control my muscles. Mamma and Papà immediately stripped me naked and started rubbing my body with alcohol. It worked. My temperature dropped and I didn't die. There are only two memories I have from those few days. In the first, my mother is spoon-feeding me, I was so debilitated that I couldn't even raise my arms. I ate a couple of orange slices. The second memory involves my father: He's giving me a CD, De Gregori's *Mira Mare* and, as he's handing it to me, his hand is shaking. In his blue eyes, there's a palpable anguish dominating over all. Even the posture of his body is different from usual: Long pauses of immobility alternate with rapid, jerky movements. The risk I might die had been warded off, but still fear had seeped between his ribs, sharpening with every breath, eroding the certainties, crushing his illusions, confining him in that terribly violent segment of life in which you understand for real that there are times when even the people you love most can die.

The samurai was the father of two small children, a boy and a girl. His wife was pregnant again: a pair of twins.

"When I'm at sea, I disconnect, detaching from everything. I prefer not to think. In this context, if you think about your family, it weakens you. Doing sports helps a lot, it helps you to reset. I grow detached until there's nothing left but me and my objective, which is to rescue people."

He didn't modify his physical stance. Back ramrod straight, arms folded across his chest.

"The first few years really were spartan. We hauled everyone in bare-handed. Nowadays we work in wetsuits, diving masks, gloves. There are necessary rules. First and foremost: Before you start boarding people, the situation must be under control. They're going to all want to rush aboard, all at the same time. They're going to shove, grab each other, clamber up. If you're not careful, they could overturn your vessel. What's more, aside from the number of people visible on deck, those boats are often crammed full belowdecks. That's why a member of our crew always boards the refugee boat and oversees operations: When one person is taken aboard the vessel from the deck, then another can be let out of the hold. It's an absolute top priority that the already precarious stability of the refugee boat be maintained as much as possible. Often, the minute they are taken aboard the patrol boat, some of them pass out. These people are tested to the very limits of endurance, they just can't take any more. When they sight you, they try to survive to the very end, pumping their veins full of the last spurt of adrenaline left in their bodies. Then, once they're aboard the boat, they collapse. We've had to tend to quite a few, reviving them aboard the patrol boat. . . ."

His tone of voice never changed, nor did the rhythm of his breathing, the pace at which his chest rose and fell. It was as if he even trained his ribcage to hold in all his anguish.

"Sometimes the refugee boats overturn. They can go under in practically no time at all. Sometimes the sea is already full of bodies when we get there. Sometimes the bodies in the waves are alive. Sometimes they aren't. Everything boils down to a matter of timing, speed, and luck. When a body goes under, first you can see it flailing, then you see nothing. It becomes nothing."

If my silence on the phone grew too protracted, my father would nod audibly. I could imagine him sitting in his armchair, in the living room, in the darkness but with his eyes shut. I could tell that he had a thousand questions in his mind, but he was holding them back, because I still wasn't done. But I was tired, I needed a break, I needed to let the flame of anxiety smolder somewhere else.

"Have you talked to Uncle Beppe?" I asked him.

"Yes."

"When?"

"Last week."

"And how did he strike you?"

"I thought he seemed to be doing better."

"Why don't you call him?" I insisted.

Papà was caught in a dead end.

"I know, you have a point."

And he allowed the silence to say what his voice couldn't manage to express. The reason he called his brother so infrequently was that he greatly feared the possibility, a reasonably concrete possibility, that he'd get bad news. In spite of the fact that they didn't live in the same city or even in the same region—Papà lives in Palermo, Uncle Beppe lives on the other side of the Strait, in Reggio Calabria, on the mainland, on the "Continent," as we islanders say of anyone who lives elsewhere, not on our island—my father preferred to remain secure in his pew of silence, using it as a bulwark against his fear of death. If bad news doesn't arrive, that's because everything is going fine, goes the old folk saying. Papà had turned it into a personal credo. That silence was padding and shield, hope and prayer.

"But if you call him, it makes Uncle Beppe happy," I drilled in.

"You have a point," he said again. His reply was a simple, slightly abashed admission.

The mistral roared, a strong, cold, northwesterly wind, and the sea before us was whipping up, and soon night would fall.

Winter shadows always descend faster.

"In one of the last rescues, by the time we arrived, all the people were already in the water. Just yet another of the many tragedies, I thought. It was a scene far too similar to so many I'd already experienced. With the second unit, we immediately launched our collective rescue tools—rafts, life vests, lifesavers—right to where we saw the greatest number of people in the water. We shouted to them to stay calm, we were going to steer away from them but we'd be back to rescue them as soon as we could. That moment is always so terrible. The minute they see you turning away, the panic sweeps over them. They freak out. They're even more likely to drown. But we couldn't just stay there. We sailed to the far ends of the shipwreck, heading in one direction while the other unit went the other way. There were people scattered over the surface of the sea for a radius of three miles."

So that's the meaning of the parable about the lost sheep, I thought. Rely on the likelihood that the rest of the flock won't drown while you try to rescue those who've been swept away by the current. There was the whole catechism that I'd studied as a child in those words. It kicked me in the head and chest, the fact that this was a concrete example. The parable, at last, had become flesh. It was all right here, in the effort made by the muscles to retrieve the bodies, in the scrupulous scanning of the waves to make sure you don't overlook even a single life, in the effort to keep your nerves steady as you haul those lost at sea to safety.

"We started hauling in people, one by one, working inward from the two extremities of the rescue field, until we met at the point where we had launched the first rafts. We rescued them all. Every last one. There were one hundred fifty-six of them. Unfortunately, we were unable to save one of them. We even did a heart massage aboard ship, but clearly, he had lost all remaining strength."

The count of the living and the count of the dead.

The origin of the anguish, the cause of the battle.

"One morning we took a young man out of the water who was no longer breathing. His heart wasn't beating. Even the doctor took him for dead. One of my men, the one who had physically rescued him at sea, claimed that he'd detected a heartbeat, had felt a faint, almost imperceptible pulse. He started giving him a heart massage. I don't know what clicked in his head, but he continued giving him that cardiac massage for the next twenty minutes without stopping, in the middle of the sea, on his return from a rescue during which we had recovered one hundred fifty-eight people alive, out of one hundred fifty-nine. And the only one who seemed not to have made it was the very person that he was trying to bring back to life, in defiance of all logic. Twenty minutes of unbroken cardiac massage. That's a tremendously long time. I really don't know where my guy found the strength to keep at it for so long. We were all amazed. And you know what? It worked. He managed to bring him back. That man who had been taken for dead came back to life. His heart started beating again. No one could believe it. The judgment of the doctor on board was: 'He brought him back to life.'"

The samurai smiled, and yet all that I could see was a shepherd thinking about his flock and suffering for that one lonely lost sheep.

"There's something that's really been bothering me, Papà."

My father's breathing had changed instantly. He'd started breathing like a doctor again. He disclosed his prognosis in the form of a question.

"Do you think he's suffering from post-traumatic stress?" he asked.

"No," I replied quickly.

"I don't know," I corrected myself.

"Maybe so, I think he might be, actually," I retracted. I really had no idea.

"His words were glimpses into the abyss. It was like talking to the veteran of a terrible war. And that fit, well-trained body, those still, unmoving eyes were a physical testimonial to the battle still under way, beyond the horizon, where an endless bloodbath is playing out. He had all the sounds and smells of war carved into his flesh. I don't know how to put it any better than that, Papà, forgive me."

"You have nothing to apologize for."

I sat down on the low wall of the veranda and I took my head in my right hand. I pressed my palm against my eyeball. I exhaled loudly, profoundly, slowly. Then I inhaled for an even longer time.

"I believe that I was appalled by the sheer quantity of death that I read on his face. He's a direct eyewitness to the darkest side of history. He and his colleagues fight every day, but not against the sea or against time. No. His is a challenge to death itself. And that sort of battle cannot help but mark your face, your flesh, your breath, your gaze."

"What feelings did he inspire in you?"

"Respect and gratitude, Papà. I felt like hugging him. But I didn't. And I'm sorry I didn't."

———

I had asked the commander of the Capitaneria di Porto what the hardest moment of his time on Lampedusa had been. I expected a story charged with tragedy and heroism, with an apocalypse on the open sea as the setting.

"The time one of our men died of a disease," was his answer. He told me about all the efforts they'd made to ensure that their colleague received the finest medical care, the searches they did for specialists, the vacation days spent going to see him at the hospital, the heartbreak of the last few days of his illness, the unconsolable grief of his family, the dismay of the whole group.

"There was no way we could have imagined he was going to die. He was a big-hearted kid, always cheerful. He was one of us."

Esprit de corps is found especially among people who live through emotionally upsetting experiences such as war. Soldiers remember the exceptional nature of the friendships established and nurtured while under arms. Those friendships are formed in a very short span. They're as luminous as a burst of flame. Under extraordinary conditions, extraordinary relationships bloom. And, in a certain sense, in a distorted way that is no less real for its twisted nature, soldiers remain tied to war or, rather, to that particular, ferocious condition that takes to its maximum intensity the ties with the other people in their group. A terrible love of war, in which you developed an unbreakable spirit of brotherhood, strengthened by the concrete fact that these men save each other's lives. Those are emotions that possess such power, such a strong charge that it can be nearly impossible to find anything like them for the rest of your life. And so, the rest of a lifetime after a war can prove not to be enough to relive the intensity of that excitement, those emotions.

It's not just love that sets a seal on the ties that bind.

Violence, too, can create them.

Πόλεμος (Polemos, the Daemon of War) is father to all things.

The crews work on what's visible, before the body is swallowed up by the water. Accustomed to saving lives, when one of them—a savior, a rescuer—dies of some disease, they are forced to admit the greater truth that we are helpless in the face of the invisible. All of the training in this world might not be enough, sometimes. Disease lurks under the surface. It takes the body from within, like some inner weight that drags you under, inexorably.

In a theology of material things, what can save you if it's matter itself that devours your life?

Is this the sense of helplessness that a doctor feels when a patient dies, when a treatment fails, when a tumor recurs, even after your brother has defeated a first case of cancer?

You look on helplessly at a shipwreck, and it's as if the water were pouring into you, too.

The samurai said: "Talking about it helps, for sure, even just to get free of the things you carry inside you. But, honestly, I never do it. Not even with my wife. Inflicting my anguish on her wouldn't be fair. She always says to me: 'You never talk to me about what happens to you at work,' but I prefer to keep her separate from it. Oh lord, I like having my children know the kind of work their father does, they're proud of it, they talk about it at school, they tell their classmates when they hear the news reported on TV. But I don't tell them anything more. Among my colleagues, we always hold a briefing after a rescue, to figure out if there was anything we could have done better. We discuss the things that happened, in and of themselves. But we don't dig any deeper. We avoid that. Now that we've built a team, in September there's going to be a changing of the guard, new personnel will come in, I'll be done with my work here, others will take my place. I'll go away, but I'll leave a family behind me, the guys I lived with, 24-7. The things we faced up to brought us together, strengthened our ties even more."

The samurai changed position. He turned to stare out at the sea. We'd reached the last chapter, the one in which the warrior bares his chest and reveals on what field the battle is really raging.

"Only once did I have a moment of weakness. On October 3 I was in the first boat to take to the sea after the alarm was received. After we rescued the living, we started pulling in the corpses that were bobbing in the water. A week later, on October 11, there was another shipwreck, in the open waters. Same situation, same heartbreak: You've already recovered lots and lots of dead people, and now the same thing happens to you again, a week later, after you thought you'd seen everything. But instead, there you are, reliving the same exact scene."

Training, team spirit, pride—none of it was any help now.

His chest was exposed.

My heart, my heart, how many bolts must still pierce you?

"The ones we went out onto the open sea to rescue on October 11 were Syrians . . . there was a little girl in the water . . . the spitting image of my own daughter . . . she was floating in the water . . . I took her in my arms . . . she was identical . . . at that instant I found myself experiencing that situation . . . she was the same as my daughter . . . the same haircut . . . the same facial features . . . it really upset me . . . I couldn't move for a couple of minutes . . . she was identical to my daughter . . . I forced myself not to think about it again . . . never again. . . ."

The sun had started to set along the horizon line.

"What will you do far from here?"

"I'll spend time with my family. I'll sail in the waters off my home."

"You just can't stay away from the water."

"It's my job, but that's not all. I really have an enormous respect for the sea. The most beautiful things I've seen in my life are sunset and sunrise over the water, light so intense that it just makes you appreciate our profession even more. Sometimes I say to myself: This is one of the reasons I did this, to preserve in my memory these snapshots that remain inside me over the course of time."

When it came time to say goodbye, I bowed my head slightly, the way they do in Japan. That is how you salute a warrior.

Darkness had fallen over Cala Pisana.

The sky was covered with clouds.

There was no glitter of even a single star.

There were no lamp-fishing boats out on the water.

No light in front of my eyes.

"You did right by getting him to speak."

My father's declaration caught me off guard.

"You think?"

"Yes."

It was a cracked-open door, a rope tossed in my direction, a way of asking: "Let me speak, too."

He would have liked to use me, his son, as a father, or even as an elder brother. But all around me was the darkness of winter and I was a complete wreck.

"Papà, Melo just came out onto the veranda, dinner is ready."

My father remained silent for several seconds, too long to toss out a second call for help.

His breathing had changed once again.

Between systole and diastole, anxiety had returned.

"All right, then, ciao."

We waited a little longer, in silence, with the phones in our hands, each facing his own emptiness, like two vessels that have grazed each other, in the open sea in the dark of night, only to continue their solitary journeys.

There's one photo my father took that I love in particular. It depicts, on the top of a hill, one next to the other, a ruined building and a tree, maybe a holm oak, maybe a wild pear. It's a black-and-white shot. The sky, indifferent to goings-on below, is a motionless backdrop crisscrossed by unraveling cirrus clouds, like so many jagged rips in the canvas. Farther down, just over the edge of the hilltop, scattered white clouds create an illusion of vertigo. At first glance, it seems as if the picture were taken at quite an elevation, but there's a small dark triangle at the bottom right which reveals the presence of the sea just below, making it clear these are just hills. The points of greatest intensity in the photograph are the crown of the tree and the small window in the ruin.

In this motionless setting—just as Sicily is motionless, as the world is, and life itself—the ruin and the tree are close at hand, companions on the stage.

I'd shown the photo to Silvia.

"It's powerful."

"It makes me think about my relationship with Papà," I said.

"Certainly," she replied. And then she knocked me off balance. "You and your father had learned to keep each other company in silence, exactly like the tree and the ruin. Just think how nice it is that now your Papà uses photographs and you use the written word: You have the tools to shade each other, protect each other, leaning against each other. And maybe, if you keep it up, you'll even be able to speak to each other, the way I personally believe the tree and the ruin already do, when there are no prying eyes around."

Paola had cooked crayfish and mullet.

"You're not very hungry."

"Is it so obvious?"

"Usually you scarf down whatever I serve you."

The moon had started to pierce the clouds, which were being shredded and swept away by the mistral wind. Clouds aren't endless. Sooner or later they vanish. Outside the window, the moon was red, and its reflection was warm on the section of sea enclosed in the cove.

Paola smiled as she lit up a cigarette.

"Do you know when I really started to understand what was happening, Davidù? It was on account of a Kurd who landed on the island. You remember him, Melo?"

"Fuck, unforgettable, he was just too fantasic," Melo replied, before chugging down a whole glass of beer at a single gulp.

"He might have been forty years old or so. He was a teacher or professor of some scientific subject, maybe it was chemistry, I don't really remember that detail anymore.

He'd come over to have an espresso with us. We were laughing and joking, partly in English and partly in French. At a certain point the Kurd told us a joke. Hearing it was like having your eyes opened: In spite of everything—prison in Libya, the nightmarish sea crossing that he had undertaken, and that went on for days and days, his family abandoned back home—well, the fact that he was telling us a joke made it clear to me that these people weren't abstractions or newspaper headlines, they were actually human beings. I know that that might seem contrived, but it isn't, believe me. I also know that I don't come off particularly well, but it took a joke to make me realize that there was a completely mistaken narrative about what was happening."

Melo had made it to the sofa, while Paola's cigarette was burning away between her fingers. A long column of ash collapsed into the ashtray, puffing into dust on impact.

"Before, I instinctively saw only their burden of suffering, their malnourished bodies, the bruises, the scars, the fear in their eyes. I looked down on these people from a pedestal, you understand? From a position that meant that they, by virtue of the fact that they were being given help, are and will always be less than. But instead, at that instant, during the joke, I started to intuit the profundity of the stories of every single person who had transited through here. Certainly, I knew I couldn't fully grasp the pain of those experiences, but I had just realized that it was and is a huge mistake to treat them in such an obtusely paternalistic way. There's more, aside from desperation. There's also the yearning for redemption and a better life, there are songs and games, the desire for certain foods in particular, and the desire to play and joke with others. Anyway, so this is the joke. A Kurd dies and is sent to Hell. There he spends all his time crying and wailing. So, an angel arrives and asks him: 'Kurd, why are you crying?' The Kurd replies: 'I don't want to be here.' The angel decides to intervene: 'All right, then come with me.' And he takes the Kurd to Heaven. There, before he even has a chance to get settled in, the Kurd starts crying and wailing again, in despair, never stopping. At that point, the Good Lord shows up in person. 'Kurd, why are you crying?' He asks. And the Kurd replies: 'I don't want to be here.' And God says to him: 'Wait, so Heaven is no good either? Where do you want to go?' And the Kurd replies: 'Germany.'"

There's an expression in my dialect, *"calare 'u scuro 'mpetto"* (darkness falls in my chest), that indicates a particular state of mind: when a sense of malaise comes down from above and takes complete possession of a person. In the dialect of Palermo, the chest is a fairly extensive area of the body, ranging from the throat to the arms and farther down, below the stomach. It's the first part of a human being to impact against the things of life. It's in your chest that you feel the emotions of existence. There's your heart, for instance, which dries out. *"Mi siccò 'u cori,"* is when you discover something so painful and grievous that it zeroes out the very essence of life: water, which stops bubbling to the surface at those latitudes. When darkness falls in your chest, every aspect of existence finds itself held prisoner by deep, arid shadows. Immersed in that darkness, you can no longer believe in any possibility whatsoever of redemption, with no comet on the horizon to point the way, the escape route from that suffering.

And then there's the opposite motion, when the darkness goes away because "*'a tavola d'u petto si gràpe,*" the table of the chest opens up, and "*si gràpe puru 'u cori,*" the heart opens up, too, unhinging the rib cage while the ribs spread wide in an embrace, to let in light and air, because happiness is only happiness if it's free.

The Kurd's joke began to scatter my shadows.

"Come on, Davidù," said Melo, "stop busting our balls and have a beer with me."

I was really captivated by this way he had of interacting without filters, without calculating the consequences. I was sick and tired of mathematics in human relations.

The last time that I stayed with them at Cala Pisana, the room on the other side of the patio was occupied by a vacationing couple. The man was blind practically from birth, while the woman had been sighted until she turned ten. They had computers they used by means of voice recognition.

Until then, it had never occurred to me that blind people went on holiday all by themselves.

Melo listened to their stories openmouthed. For three days he let them talk, without saying a single word. Then, at breakfast, he asked them a direct question: "Do you guys dream?"

He'd been mulling that question for days.

"Sure," husband and wife replied in chorus, laughing, happy that there was no awkwardness.

"And what do you dream of?" Melo drilled in.

Once again, the couple answered as one.

"We dream of sounds, smells, tactile sensations."

Thanks to Melo's brash shamelessness, prospects now opened out before me that I could never before have imagined, in which a dream is a melody, it's the smell of the trunk of an olive tree you knew in your childhood, it's the softness of silk along the curve of a back, it's the cherry flavor of a kiss you'd thought long lost.

Paola had just put the evening espresso pot on the flame.

"When are you coming back here with your father?"

"Why, am I not enough just by myself?"

"No, your father is better," she and Melo replied in chorus, snickering.

"Soon, soon, maybe I'll bring my uncle, too."

I couldn't know it yet, but I would come back to Cala Pisana with Papà eleven months after that first and, till then, only trip together, for the anniversary of October 3, when people were still dying in the sea and Uncle Beppe's lymphoma had gotten worse.

———————

"What did you think of the lady doctor from CISOM?" Melo asked, cutting straight to the point. CISOM is an acronym for Corpo Italiano di Soccorso dell'Ordine di Malta—the Order of Malta's Italian Relief Corps—the civilian volunteer agency that on Lampedusa provides medical support staff on the vessels of the Italian Coast Guard and the Italian Navy. These volunteers are first responders, providing medical care while still out to sea.

"She was upset. Like everybody else I'm meeting. Like anyone who lives on this island. The same way that you two are upset."

Paola got up to turn off the espresso pot, then she brought it to the table and set it down at the center. Melo finished the beer, drinking directly from the bottle. The dining room was cozy, the cove was right in front of it, the smell of salt and brine filled the air, and I missed my father.

The doctor was named Gabriella. She was less than thirty years old. She seemed full of energy, with nice manners, and a tragedy to put behind her.

"Aboard the patrol boats there are two of us from CISOM, a doctor and a nurse. If there are no serious injuries, then we first examine the children, then the women, and last of all, the men. Very often, we see pregnant women. On one rescue, there were a great many pregnant women, at least a dozen, from their second to their eighth month of pregnancy."

Most of those pregnancies were the result of rapes.

It's always worse if you're a woman, on the wrong side of the border.

"The men usually have contusions, sprains, and fractures caused by the torture they've suffered in Libyan prisons. Some of them show signs of wounds from gunshots. We examined a young man with a crutch who'd been shot in the leg. There was no mistaking the entry and exit wounds. Legs are the parts of the body most often hit by gunshots, but I've examined young men with similar injuries to the shoulders and the arms."

Melo stood up, grabbed two beers, opened them both, and set one down in front of me.

Paola said: "I'm increasingly convinced that for doctors working humanitarian missions on the waters of the Mediterranean, conditions are similar to those found in a refugee camp in a war zone."

"You're surrounded by doctors," was what Melo came up with. "Your father, your mother, your uncle," he added.

"Cardiologist, child neuropsychiatrist, nephrologist," I reply. Ever since I was small, I've felt protected by that constant presence of doctors.

"Why didn't you become a doctor?"

"What need was there? They were already everywhere I looked."

Nothing could happen to me, everything would be diagnosed in plenty of time, everything would be cured. Perhaps that was also why I had such a hard time understanding my father's agitation about Uncle Beppe's lymphoma. He'd already had one tumor, and he'd beaten it spectacularly, fuck off, cancer, you'll never beat us: no, not the Enia family.

Gabriella said: "It was a Sunday morning in February. We weren't expecting a call, there was a force-seven gale, and there had been no reports of any vessels setting sail. We were at lunch, after attending Mass, invited by the staff of the CISOM group of Lampedusa, along with a few of the men from the Capitaneria di Porto, the port authorities, and the commander of the border patrol. When the lunch was over, the commander of the maritime district office of Lampedusa received the call: There was a rescue target one hundred thirty miles out of Lampedusa. It was very far away, and it was already three in the afternoon. We were going to have to cross the sea in terrible conditions. I was both worried and excited, it would be my first time going out. Right from the departure, a few members of the crew started getting sick, vomiting over the side. The sea was churning, the waves were enormous. During the trip, other members of the crew started getting sick. They were vomiting, too. I looked at them and I thought: How can it be that they're getting sick like this? I'm not accustomed to it, and yet I'm handling it beautifully! I tried to give them advice about the best posture to assume to reduce the nausea to a minimum, suggesting they drink plenty of water and take supplements. I offered to give shots, even though, in that gale-force sea, the movements of the patrol boat were unpredictable and there was a serious risk of hurting the patient. While we were sailing, I discovered that even the captain had a very high fever. I hadn't known it when we set out because when I boarded the ship, he was already overhead, at the bridge."

Paola continually lit and put out the lighter. The pack of cigarettes lay untouched on the table. It wasn't time for a new cigarette yet.

Melo had just finished drinking a sip of beer.

"When there are storms on the Mediterranean, it's an especially challenging environment for this type of mission," he opined.

"Simone told us that, when he came back from the Atlantic Ocean," Paola went on.

The summer had gone like that: When the high season was over, Melo had convinced Simone to try crossing the Atlantic Ocean as crew member on a sailboat.

"Upon his return from that adventure, Simone was overjoyed. He confided to us that in those two weeks he'd understood one enormous difference between the Atlantic

Ocean and the Mediterranean Sea. Here in the Mediterranean, open-water rescues are more complex because, in the stretch of sea between Lampedusa and Africa, the seabed is much shallower than it is in the ocean. In the Atlantic, the waves are very high and last for tens of seconds at a time. You see them coming with plenty of advance warning, and you ride over them. The time frame of any given wave is much more extensive. Here, instead, the waves crash down one after the other, without a break, like so many fists slamming into the hull, repeatedly from all different heights, in a continuous series of ups and downs. The Italian Coast Guard goes out in truly horrifying weather and sea conditions, but horrifying in the most absolute sense—it's not just a figure of speech."

That consideration confirmed something that everyone in town had already told me: The Italian Coast Guard goes out all the time, whatever the conditions on the water. The samurai, when I told him about that unanimous chorus about the work they did, replied: "There's that Kevin Costner movie, *The Guardian*, where at a certain point one character says about the Coast Guard: 'When storms shut down entire ports, we go out.' And it's true." And he'd followed that quotation with a long laugh, finally relaxing the musculature of his shoulders and the lines of his forehead. I had laughed with him, and I'd imagined him at his home, in front of the TV, watching that movie with his kids, talking to them about going out onto the open sea, when the storm is raging all around him and the waves are thirty feet high, a little bit minimizing, and a little bit just missing the experience.

Gabriella said: "Around ten at night we arrived at the target but we couldn't see it. It was all too dark. In the darkness, we could just catch a glimpse of the other patrol boat, which just like us was sailing back and forth, and in the distance the tugboat from the oil platform, an immense, enormous structure. While we went on searching, all the running lights were on, the waves were still very high, and everything was black. The sky was black, the sea was black. The moon, on the other hand, was enormous and beautiful. A big, full African moon. At last, we found them. They were aboard a rubber dinghy. The diver and the members of the crew started maneuvering for rescue. But then everyone aboard the rubber dinghy started jumping up and moving. They were waving their hands. They wanted to get aboard our ship right away. They were all getting agitated. We members of the CISOM set off wearing our uniform: a white T-shirt with a logo reading either CISOM PHYSICIAN or CISOM NURSE, dark-blue waterproof trousers, running shoes, and when we board the patrol boat, a white Tyvek jumpsuit, which is a pleasure to wear in the winter, though in the summer not so much. The jumpsuit has a hood and, since I was wearing that hood, I realized that the hood might be scaring the kids. I took off the hood, in part to show them that I was a woman, and I started shouting: 'Quiet! We are here to help you!' One of the leaders understood and, translating the message, had them pass it along the length of the rubber dinghy. As soon as they calmed down, they were gradually taken aboard our ship, one at a time. They were all males, one hundred four people on a single rubber dinghy. On the bow of the rubber dinghy someone had written the number 3 in magic marker. There must have been two other rubber dinghies out on the water. The report that had come in, in fact, mentioned three rubber dinghies, not just one. We never did find the other two."

Paola poured herself some water.

I was stroking the neck of the beer bottle.

I wonder how I would have interacted with Gabriella if I'd been a doctor.

Who knows what kind of questions my father would have asked her.

"There's an aspect that struck me."

Melo was thinking aloud, looking out the window at Cala Pisana.

"Her first experience of death came in absentia, not by direct presence."

The two rubber dinghies missing at sea.

Death as an evocation.

In western culture, the image certifies the reality of what exists: an event, a revolution, a death, are all to some extent amplified if captured by the eye. The things you haven't seen are to a certain extent rendered less powerful precisely because they have not been the object of your sight. Oral culture has made way for visual culture.

But the invisible goes on working way beneath the surface, far from view, delving into the innermost recesses.

The advance on tragedy takes place in silence, with an absence. What is missing not only makes the picture incomplete, it opens a gap that becomes the fracture. And it is exactly into that void that death surges.

"Our patrol boat took aboard fifty-eight people, the other forty-six boarded another vessel. I was forward, the nurse was astern. We checked them one by one. They were very young men, the oldest couldn't have been more than thirty, all of them barefoot and drenched from head to toe. We gave each of them a thermal blanket. Aside from the thermal blankets, we had a number of hot packs, little units similar to dry ice: When you break them, they instantly get very warm. We distributed all the hot packs on board. Unfortunately, there weren't enough for everyone. The ones who hadn't been given them just wrapped themselves in their thermal blankets. It was intensely cold. Once the nurse and I had determined that every single one of those young men was in good condition, I stopped to talk a while with those who were sitting along the sides of the patrol boat, asking each of them where they were from. Mali, Guinea, Gambia—basically from all over Africa. They said they were all right, even though they'd been out on the open seas for seven days and hadn't eaten in two weeks. I moved over to the far side of the patrol boat, and talked to the other young men on that side. 'Where do you come from?' I showed them the pendant on my necklace, which depicted Africa. One young man pointed to it and told me the name of his city, which was, however, a place I'd never heard of. The time had come to get moving. Before going into the cabin, I told them, in English: 'Guys, now the journey is going to be long and difficult, but don't worry, because you're strong and you'll make it.' Then I went into the cabin. And then . . . ' "

She burst into tears.

These were tears that she'd incubated for a long time.

It lurked there, behind all those words.

It was the shadow of the words.

The origin of the Calvary.

Beneath the ashes of time smolder the embers of regret.

"It took us a very long time to reach Lampedusa. Those were the longest hours of my life. Outside it was unimaginably cold, twenty-five-foot waves, force-eight winds, a raging gale, and these young men were freezing. They couldn't come into the cabin. Inside, the crew members were sick as dogs, constantly vomiting. I did my best to get to a secure position, as a physician I knew I'd have to act if anyone's condition worsened. I remember this scene: The cabin door was still open, and heads started to poke through it. I counted them. There were ten of them. The young men wanted to come in because they were suffering from the cold. I asked: 'Why don't we let them come in, at least a few of them?' I was told: 'That's not possible. There could be a mutiny.' The door was shut. But outside they were freezing, the rain was pouring down, the wind was howling, there was everything imaginable and more. The young men banded together and tried to force the door. A young man outside the door kept saying he'd had an operation. 'Operated! Operated!' he kept shouting, 'Operated!' He never said anything else. The diver and a crew member tried to get the door shut again, doing their best not to crush their hands, which they'd forced in through the gap in the door. One of the crew lost his temper and started shouting at the boys, barking at them to stay outside. Those bellowing orders upset me. Later, when I thought it over, I realized that that angry reaction sprang from the frustration of being unable to do as much to help them as we might want. We were all in a state of emergency, the whole situation was really harsh. It was a way of venting against an entire violent system of which they themselves had been victims. The door was forced shut again. The hours went by, the crew members kept getting sick, the waves tossed us up and down, and outside it was still incredibly cold. The commander reached out to the commander of the other patrol boat for information, who replied that aboard his boat the young men had been allowed to enter the cabin, taking turns. So, our commander decided to do the same thing. We established shifts and let six young men come into the cabin, packed tight. That was the largest number who could fit in there. Around three in the morning, the engineer went on deck, emerging directly from the engine room door. When he came back inside, these were his words: 'There are at least four or five of them dead, in the bow.' The world collapsed around me. I was a doctor, I'd been there to help them and get them all back home safe and sound, and I hadn't been able to do anything for them. The diver said: 'I'm going out to see what condition they're in.' Divers have a hook that allows them to anchor themselves to the patrol boat, which means they're not at risk of being swept overboard. When he returned, he confirmed that there was nothing to be done, they were unresponsive, they really were dead. Around two in the afternoon, the engineer reported that still more of them had died. I felt even more useless and helpless. We reached Lampedusa around five in the afternoon. Twenty-nine of the young men were dead.

"During the trip back, I'd tried repeatedly to find the strength. To stay awake. I was drinking lots of water. I never threw up at all. But my mental lucidity came and went. I was troubled by extreme thoughts. In order to find strength and courage, I would think of a green meadow. And I felt guilty, because the others were outside suffering from the cold, while I was struggling to visualize that image. I prayed from start to finish. As soon as we tied up to the wharf, I got up from where I was sitting, doing my best to gather my strength, all the strength that remained to me. Right outside of the cabin, I saw the young man who had shouted, 'Operated!' He was sprawled on the deck, his head next to the ladder...motionless...beside him there were others...a great many others...one atop the other...naked, like in a film that I saw about Auschwitz, *Son of Saul*...most of them had no clothing...trousers pulled down, T-shirts hiked up...genitals on display...supine and prone...heaps of bodies....One young man in the bow recognized a friend among the corpses, perhaps a relative. As he looked at the body, he froze to the spot and started to cry. He didn't want to leave that body there. There was such a sad expression on his face, as if he didn't want to be saved anymore. I disembarked from the patrol boat. On the Molo Favaloro, a female doctor I knew came toward me. I remember that I only realized I'd landed when she called me by my name, 'Gabriella.' It was as if at that moment I had awakened from a nightmare. 'What happened?' she asked me. She would often talk to me about the concept of '*nuda vita*' (naked life) in the work of the philosopher Giorgio Agamben. 'Look, that is naked life, which you've told me so much about....There, those are bodies, they're nothing but bodies.' A volunteer from the welcome center came over to try to comfort me. I told him: 'This was my first mission, and look what happened....' They accompanied me and the nurse to another ship, larger than the patrol boat. There they brought us hot tea and let us catch our breath. We hadn't had anything to drink or to eat in a day. Through the porthole I looked out at the dead bodies on the wharf, covered by a green tarp. At last I found the strength to cry."

"It's not always this way. When you talk to other people they'll tell you that they had a very different experience. I still wonder why this thing happened to me of all people. But I'm working on it. There have been other boat-to-boat transfers since. Fortunately, they were all all right...the pregnant women...the children...it all went fine...the weather conditions were certainly much better."

"Not many have understood the grief I still carry within me. Twenty-nine dead. Half of the fifty-eight who boarded our patrol boat. It wasn't four, it wasn't five, it wasn't six. It was twenty-nine. Every day is a new loss."

ONE OF THOSE BLESSED PAUSES had come to the island where you could no longer hear the scream of the mistral wind.

"Everything passes, the winds, the winter, the travails of life," said Melo.

"I like the sound of the waves going out," I put in.

"The sea always keeps us company, even when it's too cold to go swimming," Paola added.

"Hell, what are we turning into? The school of philosophy?" said Melo stretching out on the sofa, lifting his forearm to cover his brow.

Bedtime was drawing closer.

The muscles of my back, tensed until then, finally began to relax.

"You know, before coming back here, this afternoon I talked a little with a crew member from the patrol boats. He showed me a video he took on board with his cell phone, right after a rescue. In the stern, they had the young people they'd just recovered, all of them male. There were about a hundred of them. He'd told me that they found them early in the morning, all aboard a single rubber dinghy, and when they intercepted them, the water had already risen to their crotches. His exact words were these: Another couple of minutes and we'd have lost them forever. In the video, which is no longer than thirty seconds, if that, the scene is apparently absurd, because we're on the patrol boat that's sailing in the open sea on its way back to Lampedusa, and in the stern are all these kids who just came close to dying and in the background you can hear loud and clear, live, some kind of Latin American music. What had happened was this: The chief engineer had gone up to the bridge and placed his cell phone, with a recording of this Latin American song, against the microphone of the intercom, so that it played all over the deck. At the center of the frame was the crew member I'd spoken to, seen from behind, with all the rescued kids in front of him, busy coordinating a complicated dance choreography, as if he were an event supervisor at some resort village, and they're all moving their arms and hands in time to the music, swinging left and right, up and down. And all the rescued kids are replicating his moves, dancing, laughing, and singing along. I found this little video to be deeply moving. There was such purity in that manifestation of joy, and such tact in how they convinced them to dance, that it left me speechless. Certainly, those kids were rescued in good conditions, and they were capable of moving, of course, but it was all too clear that they desperately needed to let off steam, pushing away the fear they'd built up at narrowly averting death, missing it by no more than a couple of minutes."

"It makes me think of the *picciriddo* in the fable who says: 'The emperor has no clothes,'" said Paola. "Too often we talk about human beings as numbers or statistics, instead people are much more than that, they have their hopes and prayers, their worries and their torments. So beating out the rhythm with your feet on a vessel in the open sea and clenching your fists against the sky strikes me not only as the right thing to do, but also and especially human."

"And for once, for a couple of minutes, what was fucked was death. On this round, the Lady in Black is left empty-handed," Melo summarized.

Paola lit a cigarette, leaving the lighter standing next to the ashtray.

"Are you leaving tomorrow?" she asked me.

"Yes, I have the first flight, departure at six twenty in the morning."

I was looking out to sea. I could no longer get it out of my head that somewhere, a new refugee boat had launched and a new battle was about to commence, far from the eyes of ordinary people, just over the horizon.

Melo got up from the sofa.

"Shouldn't we have a nice limoncello, to bury this day once and for all? A nice slap in the face of death. There's also an excellent wild fennel liqueur that Paola made."

"Come on, I'll have some of that."

Melo brought the bottles of liquor to the table.

"We gathered all the fennel right here," Paola insisted on pointing out.

Only a very few plants grow on Lampedusa, that was the added value.

I poured a glass but didn't drink it, letting it reach room temperature.

We sat there, listening to the sound of the waves on the sand, while the night entered the room.

"WHY DON'T YOU GO to see your uncle?"

Silvia had asked the question, looking up suddenly from the *Duino Elegies*, while I was cleaning the cuttlefish.

I stood there, frozen, with the knife in my hand.

"You always go to Lampedusa, you could at least take a trip to see him, seeing that you talk all the time. If he could see you in person, it would make him happy and you might be happier, too."

The cuttlefish lay sliced open on the cutting board, the sac with the ink was just waiting to be removed.

"You could talk face-to-face and you'd also see how he spends his days."

I set down the knife and turned on the faucet to rinse my hands. I stood there thinking, my hands under the running water, offering Silvia nothing more than that absence of words. Did I need any more evidence to make me see just how similar I was to my father?

But Silvia understood the true dimensions of that silence.

It had deep roots, which sank directly into the well of anguish.

"What's kept you from going to see him before this?"

I dried my hands. I felt my nostrils flare, the air filling my chest, my teeth clenching.

"I'm afraid."

Shivers were running down my spine, climbing up from my loins, well past my shoulder blades.

Silvia set down her book and came to hug me from behind.

"Afraid of what?"

The palms of her hands were caressing the nape of my neck, my eyes, my temples.

"Of reading a bellwether of death in his body."

She placed a quick kiss on my neck.

"If you don't see him in person, then you'll never know."

The sac with the black ink was still there, in the heart of the cuttlefish.

I gave Silvia a kiss, I turned back to the cutting board, I picked up the knife again.

"That's true."

I let the blade slice through the white flesh of the sea creature, placing it just under the membrane containing the ink.

"Do you want me to come, too?" Silvia asked, already back on the sofa, with Rilke's poetry again resting in her lap.

It would just take a short, sharp movement now, a clean cut that didn't go astray.

One.

Two.

Three.

"Yes."

The ink sac had been removed.

"Ciao, Uncle, how are you?"

"Like any old person. Are you still on Lampedusa?"

"No, I came back last week."

"Are you writing?"

"Yes."

"Hurry up and write, take it from me, because I want to read it."

"Of course. How were your exams?"

"My white blood cell count is low, but I'm still going to beat this tumor. I'm training every day, I'm lifting weights and working out on the stationary bicycle."

"Excellent. Did my father call you?"

"No. Did he call you?"

"Me neither. Zero to zero, Beppuzzo. Listen, what do you say if Silvia and I come to see you this weekend in Reggio?"

"That would be wonderful."

WE WERE AT CALA ROSSA, me, my father, Uncle Beppe, and my brother Giuseppe (who was named after Uncle Beppe, *Beppe* being the nickname for *Giuseppe* in Italian). Papà was leading the line as we made our way in single file down the steep path between the rocks to get down to the sea. Uncle Beppe brought up the rear. In his calm voice, addressing me and my brother, he'd admonished us: "Children, careful not to fall." And an instant later—literally, a fraction of a second later—his feet lost their grip on the soil, his right sandal flew into the air, and Uncle went skidding dangerously down the rocks, vanishing behind a boulder. Everyone present, a dozen people, burst out laughing, including me and my brother. Even my father, who had immediately turned around to make sure he wasn't hurt, couldn't manage to wipe the smile off his face. We saw Uncle Beppe's hand reach out from behind the rock. His clenched fist slowly changed shape: The raised thumb was the sign that Uncle had chosen to communicate the fact that he was still alive. Then we heard his voice. "Children, don't worry, I didn't get hurt at all." And at last, he emerged from that landscape of thorns and stones. His T-shirt was all torn, his right thigh was badly scratched, an abrasion ran from his left buttock all the way down to his ankle. Everyone who was present, when they saw him get to his feet, burst into a sincere round of thunderous applause. My uncle blushed instantly, and in order to get out of that moment of embarrassment, started to make a benediction, using the first three fingers of his hand. He looked like the pope. We all returned that improvised benediction with small nods of the head, then each of us went back to enjoying our day.

"Do you feel like continuing on down?" my father asked him.

"Sure," my uncle muttered. When he noticed how badly torn his T-shirt was, he declared, unable to stifle a smile: "Oh well, it was a miserable shirt to start with." He waded in and cleansed his wounds with salt water. "Damn, I fell down," he kept saying, to me, to my brother, to my father, to himself, laughing even before anybody else thought of it. It was a beautiful morning, bright and sunny, and Papà was swimming offshore, Uncle Beppe was keeping an eye out to make sure that my brother didn't drown, while I retrieved three sea urchin skeletons, diving with my mask. It was August of 1981, the family car was a beige Fiat Panda, and Uncle Beppe was living in England, where he was specializing in nephrology.

"In those days, nephrology was a growing medical science, we were like pioneers when I decided to specialize in it. It was the future, just like my other great passion, molecular biology. I became a doctor because I was attracted by the dynamics of the body. Certainly, a considerable influence on my decision came from the fact that my brother had already been studying medicine for the previous four years. It was like seeing a sign pointing me in the direction of the road to follow."

Beppe and I went back to Cala Rossa in 1987. My uncle—who had come to Palermo for the summer holiday from Reggio Calabria, where he had moved for work a couple of years earlier—had driven me to a soccer match. I was the classic thirteen-year-old boy: pimply, awkward, constant erections. What's more, I was already considered to be a pretty good soccer player. The opposing team was a player short, so they asked my uncle if he wanted to play on their side.

"If you play, we're eleven against eleven, come on, will you do us the favor?"

He agreed. That was fine with me, my uncle was a very mediocre player, they were certain to put him out in the field on defense, that's what happens to mediocre players, and since I was a striker, a left fielder, I was going to clean up, I'd aim at him systematically, getting him drunk on feints and false moves, and I was sure to score goal after goal. It promised to be an exhilarating afternoon. I didn't just want to beat him, I really wanted to humiliate him.

I'll never forget that match.

Uncle Beppe decided to play an epic game. No question, he was an awkward player and awkward he remained, but he was unexpectedly, damnably effective. He denied every concluding shot I tried to drive in, he anticipated whatever move I tried on, he'd shatter our plays at the line of attack with moves that were aesthetically questionable but impeccable in terms of the game. He was a dam, holding us back, four-eyed and as awkward as a duck. My irritation at that outcome—the untouched nets of the opposing goal, a scoreless game that my uncle was doing his best to keep intact with an eminently respectable performance—was only increasing from one minute to the next. Until, just as the first half was coming to an end, when the zero-to-zero score seemed as solid as the nails in Jesus Christ's hands on the cross, the unthinkable happened. Uncle Beppe found the ball between his feet, and my team all on the attack. Without even stopping to think, he kicked the ball as far away as possible, trying for a safety. He gave a kick with the tip of his toe, seemingly at random, without even bothering to look at the field or his adversaries, indifferent to the summer. And that completely ignorant kick was suddenly transformed into a perfect assist, rising high over the head of our defender, until it was seized by the opposing center forward who delivered a low fastball that caught us completely off guard. One to zero, their favor. I don't know which was greater, my disappointment or my astonishment. Uncle Beppe kept laughing and saying over and over to his jubilant teammates: "I have no idea how I pulled that off." The fifteen minutes of break seemed to go on forever. I could hear the seconds ticking past. They were thorns puncturing my pride. I couldn't wait to get back on the field. I had to annihilate Beppuzzo. I couldn't lose to such an inadequate player. I was determined to be the king of the summer of 1987. The match resumed but there seemed to be no way to modify the course of events: My performance continued to be disastrous. My uncle was grinding me under in every area of the field. And yet I was a good player, and everybody knew it: "When Davidù gets the ball between his feet, he's a professor," they would say about me on the piazza. But that day the ball had decided to treat me with open hostility. I flubbed it every time I got control of it, I constantly wound up offside, and I was systematically beaten to the punch by my uncle, leaving me isolated from the flow of the game. Anger and frustration competed for the scepter of my heart. In a moment of exhaustion, in order to catch his breath, the opposing team's midfielder made a back pass, giving the ball to none other than my uncle. It was a tiny sliver of time in which I clearly read a surge of terror in Beppe's eyes. He knew that I was about to be transformed into a falcon, and that I would plummet onto that sphere, making it vanish with a magic sweep of my left foot, and then I'd gallop straight toward the glory of a certain counterattack and ensuing goal. And it would all be his fault. My uncle was a goner, my talons were spread and ready to slash. The leather sphere wound up between his feet and, exactly as had been theorized, he fell victim to a panic attack, tripped over the ball, and slid to the ground. There was nothing but open field between the young falcon and the leather ball. I was going to seize it, I'd veer around the goalie hurrying to meet me, and I'd score the point to even up the game. God, what a magnificent day I was about to give as a gift to everyone. My friends would now treat me with honor and respect. I ran head down, pumping my legs as fast as they would go. Uncle Beppe, in the meantime, doing his best to recover from the disaster he'd just triggered, stretched his leg out in front of him as he slid toward the ball. There was no way he had a chance of getting contact with the ball. I was faster than him. I was technically more skillful than him. I was stronger than him. That ball was going to be mine. I reached out my foot and—even today I still wonder how it ever could have happened, and still today I can't come up with an answer—I kicked at empty air. The tip of my shoe connected with nothing. From his position flat on the ground, Uncle Beppe had managed to get his foot on the ball before I had. It was a matter of inches, really, but those few inches meant my reign over the summer was still-born, unachieved. Ice gripped my heart. Unfortunately for me, it still wasn't over. There are always conditions that can transmute a loss into a crushing defeat without mitigating circumstances. Just think of the worst. And it will happen. And back on that day in 1987, the worst did happen. This is how it went: Uncle Beppe didn't just prevent my counterattack. With that miserable kick he managed to achieve the absolute exploit designed to humiliate another human being in the most supreme manner imaginable on the soccer field. My uncle pulled a tunnel. On me. His favorite nephew. The promising rising star of the new arrivals to the soccer season, the children of 1974. My legs stood by, helpless and disconcerted, as the ball trotted carefree through them. My body had been transformed into a right of way, a tunnel. He'd pulled off a textbook demonstration of the tunnel. By now the ball was behind me, a good ten feet behind my back. The whole opposing team had exploded in a deafening roar. I could not believe it. I was so ashamed that my ears blazed red. It was the end of me as a soccer player. I was a promise broken. And so I gave the worst of myself. I collapsed, body and soul, into a hysterical fit, cursing like a lunatic at my bad luck and at the pounded dirt that had sent the bouncing ball astray. I left the field, abandoning my team on the verge of an enemy goal. I walked toward the water without a word to anyone. I believe that my plan was to swim out to the horizon until I touched land again in Liguria or Naples. Uncle Beppe came after me. I knew that he was following me. I could hear his awkward footsteps kicking the stones and scuffing up the soil. I hunkered down on a shoal of rock and waited for him. After all, it would be in his car that I'd have to travel back to Palermo. When he reached me, he stood a whole minute without speaking behind me. Then he finally found his voice.

"What kind of man do you want to be when you grow up?"

That's how he began.

"Starting today, you're choosing what type of man you want to become."

His voice was gentle.

I stubbornly remained silent. I knew that I'd behaved badly. The humiliation was stripping the flesh from my bones.

"You have to choose what you want to become, Davidù, whether you want to be a man or a *quaquaraquà*."

When I read Leonardo Sciascia's *The Day of the Owl* and saw for the first time the word *quaquaraquà*, my heart filled to bursting. My uncle had relied on the words of his favorite author to give me that advice.

"Answer me, please. What do you want to be? A man or a *quaquaraquà*?"

"A man," I muttered. My mouth was pressed against my knees. It was the only way I could think of to keep from bursting into tears.

"If you want to be a man, then start acting like one, right away."

He stood up. "I'm going back to play in that match." He patted my head, he walked back. I took one last look at the sea. My eyes were streaming tears and I was clenching my teeth to keep from sobbing. I went running back to the field. They were still playing, there were fifteen minutes of play left. We could still even up the score and, why not, we might even be able to win. I played very badly. In the last minute of play, that day went from being just incredible to outright legendary. On a corner kick, after the ball was pushed back by our defense, Uncle Beppe, in an attempt to cross the ball, actually kicked it into an off-kilter trajectory that sailed over our whole area, finally popping into the net just under the bar.

Another goal.

Two to nothing.

His teammates carried him in triumph.

Shy and embarrassed, Uncle Beppe was laughing.

"Jesus, kids, this is the first goal I've scored in my life!"

UNCLE BEPPE CAME TO PICK US UP at the station. Aunt Silvana, his wife, was still out of town for work. There was a new archaeological site in Gerace that would soon be inaugurated and she, an archaeologist, was battling against the unfailing last-minute snags and problems. But she'd be back for dinner.

When we saw each other, Uncle and I held each other in a long hug.

"You were both so sweet," Silvia confided to me later. "It's rare to see two men embrace like that in the South."

My uncle had lost weight and was wearing a baseball cap. The chemo had made his hair fall out.

"Anyway, you'd never had much hair up top."

"Asshole."

And he hugged me even harder. I could feel his fingers dig into my flesh, powerfully, the way you might grip onto a rock to keep the riptide from dragging you out to sea.

At home, Uncle immediately showed us his office where he'd set up a stationary bicycle and a treadmill. Scattered on the floor were tiny colorful fish.

"This is where I do my training. I'm going to screw the cancer once and for all."

And he laughed, with that way he had of laughing just like a kid who has gotten away with something reckless.

Outside, on the big balcony that ran all the way around the house, he took us to see his favorite plant, a frangipani.

"Look at the flowers! And this isn't even the season."

He was bursting with pride.

"My uncle Rocco gave it to me, years and years ago. It just keeps producing blooms without stopping. It really is an incredible plant."

He looked at us, seeking our approval.

"Yes, it's beautiful," Silvia replied, brushing the white petals of the flower with two fingers.

"You know, Daviduzzo, during this illness, I'm realizing how fundamental it is for a doctor to listen. I could be blind and go on practicing my profession, I swear to you, but I wouldn't be able to work if I was deaf."

My uncle stared at me, with his big, kind eyes. Dark and motionless, they were eyes you could trust.

"Listening is fundamental," he said once again, more to himself than to me. He raised his hands to his heart and started to caress them, as if he really did need that warmth in order to be able to express himself. His respiration had become labored, his pupils had narrowed. He was about to mention something painful, replicating the physical posture of his brother, my father, and my own—three separate human beings, with a shamelessly identical physical vocabulary.

"My hematologist doesn't listen to me. I tell her: My body is tired, I can feel my body give me specific instructions. But she doesn't listen to me, she just looks at the tests and already knows what to prescribe for me. Maybe she's right, of course she's certainly right, but she doesn't listen to me."

Medicine is matter acting on the body. The body is a meter of our earthly presence. It's in the flesh that disease is consummated. But there also exists, even during treatment, the whole immaterial part of the human being. And, unless you fill it up at least a little, that is the void.

Asking for help and not being listened to.

Feeling misunderstood.

Living alone in a dark room.

Is that what you feel when the pain pierces you, Uncle?

A cultural mediator who had worked at the Center in Lampedusa told me about this young boy, who'd landed only three days before, and who hadn't answered any of the standard questions asked by the people in charge of welcoming people to the Center: He wouldn't tell them his name, he wouldn't tell them what country he came from, he wouldn't tell them his age. He displayed signs of extreme anxiety. He wouldn't sleep, he wouldn't eat, he wouldn't speak to anyone. He spent his days sitting on the ground, his back against the wall, his head resting in his hands. Back then, there were only two mediators, and they couldn't keep up with everyone. In the past two weeks there had been an average of a hundred fifty people landing every thirty-six hours, and three exceptional landings with more than five hundred people each. On the fourth day, no one saw the kid around. He must have gotten out through the hole, the mediator decided. And he was right. He found him that afternoon in the piazza in front of the church. He went over to him and tried to talk to him again. He asked him his name and where he was from, and again the kid refused to answer. At that point, the mediator decided to try a different strategy; after all, he had time on his hands and there was no one there but the two of them. He asked the boy if he spoke English. The boy nodded his head yes. They'd established their first communication. And so now he asked the kid what he wanted more than anything else in the world at that moment, promising that he'd do his best to help his wish come true. I want to call home, the boy replied, I want to tell my mother that I'm still alive. He hadn't spoken to her since the day he left, eight months ago. The kid was just twelve years old.

———————

Uncle Beppe looked at his hands as he ran one slowly over the other. The rhythm of the caress proceeded in time with his breathing.

"I've always forced myself to look my patients right in the eye. Nowadays, unfortunately, the relationship with the patient is modified by the fact that, in order to speed up the procedure, the doctor spends much of his time transcribing onto a computer all the information that the patient gives him. During an office visit, a doctor spends seventy percent of his time staring at a screen. And I think that this is a problem that many doctors still haven't noticed. Even if it isn't necessary, I do my office visits the old-fashioned way: I listen to my patient's chest with the stethoscope, I check his blood pressure—a procedure that these days is performed solely by nurses—I establish that relationship of physical contact between physician and patient that I consider so important. Many of my patients have noticed this and they say to me: "Do you know how long it's been since a doctor did an old-fashioned physical examination?! Just like in the old days, what a great thing!" This makes it possible for me to talk to them. Or, really, I should say, to ask questions and listen to the answers, which is how you establish a relationship."

A kind phrase, a handshake, an ear to listen to your venting. That too is a way of healing.

———————

We spent the whole two days in Reggio Calabria at home, unless you count a short walk to get gelato on the waterfront embarcadero. There Uncle repeated the same tired line he used every time: "They call this the most beautiful mile in Italy, and you know why? Because you can see Sicily." There it was, right in front of us, disquieting and majestic, our Sicily. We'd always had a bond in our arcane, heartbroken love for our mother island. A quiver of the body, a heartbeat deeper than any other, the certain knowledge that we were islands, anywhere in the world we might be. A trait that makes brothers even of people who share no blood.

The only thing missing to make the day perfect was my father.

"It happened at night. I woke up with my back on fire, it seemed to be a problem with my lumbar vertebrae. I burned all over. I went the very next day to do some exams. And in the end, the answer was pitiless. They were lymph nodes that were compressing, it was a lymphoma. At times I have drops in my white blood cell counts. The medicines that they prescribe to increase those counts are really very strong. But I work out every day. Stationary bicycle, weights, treadmill. Let's go water the frangipani."

———

"HAVE YOU MET YOUNG MEN who landed on Lampedusa?"

My uncle had sat down on the sofa first thing in the morning and he hadn't gotten up since. Every now and then, he'd take his temperature and check the thermometer. He'd read it, and then he'd ask me to double-check for him, in case his eyes had deceived him. It was steady: 96.2 degrees. A couple of times he asked Silvia, too. "She can read it better than you can," he'd said with a laugh.

"Yes, Uncle, I've met a few."

"Poor kids, what a terrible experience that must have been."

And he sank into a rapt silence, his head nodding back and forth, his eyes closed, absolutely focused on listening.

This was the third time that Bemnet had been on Lampedusa.

The last two trips had been by plane.

They were return journeys.

The first time, he'd landed there, shipwrecked.

He had been accompanied by a couple, Denise and Peter, whom he'd met in Switzerland in 2011, when he was sleeping in a center for refugees, an old air raid shelter. The woman quickly realized just how troubled that young man was, and she helped him to start a course of therapy with a psychologist, so he could face up to his own life story.

———

Bemnet said: "Lampedusa is home, this is the place where I was reborn."

He had fled Eritrea on December 13, 2008 to avoid the draft, mandatory military service that lasts indefinitely. His mother and the other inhabitants of the village had managed to put together a substantial sum, hoping it would be enough to get Bemnet to Europe.

He'd left everything behind him: his family, his home, his friends, the things he knew, familiar faces, well-known horizons. Bemnet left knowing that he'd never again see anyone or anything he knew.

He hadn't even turned seventeen yet.

When I met him, on the beach of Rabbit Island, he was eating an apple. He really liked apples. Before coming to Europe, he'd only ever eaten one. It was when he was twelve, and his mother had gone to Asmara to buy it for him at the market.

From Eritrea, he'd walked all the way to the Sudanese border. There, in order to cross the Sahara, the traffickers had loaded them all onto jeeps. They did the trip in various legs.

At every stop, there was more money to be paid. You could keep on going till you ran out of money. When you did, they'd abandon you in the desert.

The Sahara is like the Mediterranean, full of the bones of those who were on the run and tried to cross it. Those who have no money try to challenge the desert by crossing it on foot, armed with nothing but their clothing and a bottle of water that invariably runs out far too soon. They proceed in groups. Groups that crumble like a mosaic, losing pieces. The very few who have managed to cross the desert on foot say that it's a silent journey, the group is made up of strangers, they all speak different languages, no one wants to waste saliva. They are processions that contain a vast sampling of humanity, people of all ages and social conditions. When one of them falls, if he's still alive, the others help him to his feet. If he's dead, the others take his money, if he has any hidden on his person, his shoes, if they're in better shape than the shoes they're currently wearing, his clothing, because a shirt rolled up on your head can protect you from the blast of the sun, and a belt can be sold in Libya to scrape together the money necessary to pay for the crossing. Often corpses are left behind stark naked on the sand.

After weeks in the Sahara, they reached Libya. Bemnet had run out of money. He could no longer afford a seat on a refugee boat. He was confined for months to an apartment, forbidden to go outside. Three bedrooms, a galley kitchen, a bathroom. Four hundred and fifty square feet, all told. In his room, seven men slept, at times ten, or even fifteen, always and only men. They ate what the others gave them. There was just one window. It was in the biggest room but it looked out onto a wall.

The traffickers must have understood that Bemnet would never, ever be able to scrape together the money to pay his way across the water. They could have just killed him, but instead, for no real good reason, they decided to let him board anyway.

They set sail from a Libyan beach on July 29, 2009.
There were eighty of them on a single rubber dinghy.
By now, they all more or less knew each other.

"We were like a family. We ran out of gas almost immediately. We were somewhere in the open waters, being pushed who knows where by the currents. Three days went by, with our rubber dinghy drifting helplessly. We'd run out of water and food. The sun was a form of torture. Our heads and our bodies got drenched over and over again with salt water. It was as if our flesh was on fire. Our skin was burning. Our heads felt as though they were exploding."

———————

A few people tried to paddle, reaching their arms out over the sides of the dinghy. A few people dove in, doing their best to tow the dinghy behind them as they swam.

A forty-year-old man told Bemnet that the smart thing was not to jump into the sea, not to use your arms to paddle, just to stay still, to conserve all the energy you had, not to waste your strength.

It almost sounded like an order.

Bemnet decided to follow that advice.

There were some whose throats were so dry they were coughing up blood.

There were others who, out of their minds with thirst, drank sea water.

The first retching began, followed by the first spurts of vomit, inside and outside of the rubber dinghy.

Then there were the first cases of hallucinations and the first few passengers passed out.

"To keep from dying, we started to drink our own urine. We'd urinate into a plastic bottle, into a tub, and into a plastic bag. We'd keep it. We'd share it equally."

They never did manage to get the urine to cool down. They even tried to immerse the plastic bottle in the water that had splashed into the rubber dinghy. It was no good. The urine stubbornly stayed warm.

"And then people started to die."

If someone hadn't moved in the past few hours, they'd be shaken repeatedly, for minutes at a time. It was necessary to understand whether the person was dead or had simply passed out. If someone didn't react to that persistent shaking, they'd be gently eased into the sea water.

They started praying and doing mental exercises to keep from forgetting the names of those who hadn't made it.

Various different accounts feature the same detail: Those who are drowning often shout their own name. In some cases, it's someone tossed still alive into the waves by the people smugglers. Or else it might be someone knocked into the sea by a badly broached wave. As they drown, they shout out their names.

"Why?" I'd asked.

"So they wouldn't be forgotten, no doubt about it. And to ensure that back home, the relatives and the people in the village should know that he, that name, hadn't made it, that they'd died at sea. That way, in the future they wouldn't try to track him down, they'd be freed of that apprehension."

"On the rubber dinghy, we were suffering from hallucinations. We'd lost track of the days and lost count of the
dead. No vessel intercepted us. I was paralyzed from the
belt down. I could no longer feel my legs. The sun was too
bright. I didn't even have the strength to dip my hand in the
water and wet my head. I knew everyone on that dinghy, but
I still felt desperately alone. The dead bodies were still in the
dinghy. The corpses were starting to swell. The body would
deform. The flesh would crack. We had no idea what was
happening around us. How many had died? Who was still
alive? There must have been a lot of deaths, more than half
of us, because we could sit in the bottom of the dinghy with
our legs sticking straight out. If there was room, that meant
there were that many fewer bodies. Right?"

He had two dreams. In the first one, he was in a coffin, and
standing all around him, dressed as sorcerers and priests,
were the men of the village, including his father. They were
all watching him and he, confined in the coffin, couldn't
open his eyes. He tried and tried to raise his eyelids, with
all the strength he could muster. But every single time he
failed. And yet, despite his closed eyes, in some arcane and
mysterious fashion, his father, and he alone, knew that his
son was still alive.

In the second dream, he and his friends were in a boat
and they were sailing past a village, set a little higher than

they were. But the current was so strong that it kept dragging the boat along, and that village moved away, vanishing forever.

A vessel finally did really arrive.

"It was a Maltese patrol boat. They approached, tossed us water, biscuits, a tank of gas, and then immediately veered away and roared off. No one tried to board the dinghy. I've spent years wondering why they cut and ran like that, fleeing so suddenly, trying to understand, to decipher the reason. I thought and thought, and finally came up with an answer: It was the stench of the rotting corpses in our dinghy that kept them away."

They'd spent eighteen days in the open water.

Somehow, they managed to drink and eat the provisions that had been tossed into their dinghy, they poured the gas into the tank, they eased their dead into the sea, and they set out on their course.

The Maltese patrol boat hadn't disappeared. They were sailing along, at a safe distance but still within sight. They escorted them into Italian waters, then they turned and really, finally left.

They were alone once again.

The days continued to pass.

"We were about to run out of water once again, we couldn't see land. Our strength could no longer seem to stay in our bodies."

They lived drifting across the face of the sea for three more days. Then the Italian Coast Guard arrived. They rescued them, took them aboard, and transported them to Lampedusa.

"I touched dry land on August 20. That day became my second birthday. I was reborn here."

Twenty-one days of shipwreck.

Eighty of them set out.

Seventy-five of them died.

"I don't know why I survived. I'm one of the last five who saw these people alive and yet, if I went back to my village, I really wouldn't know how to tell the story of their death. I was only seventeen years old."

Bemnet pointed to the sea.

"All my friends are out there."

He said nothing more.

————

IT WASN'T EVEN LUNCH time. Sicily was right in front of the sofa where Beppe had sat down to listen to me. Framed by the window, the island looked like a votive shrine. A benign deity in which to place your trust.

"I'm going to lie down for a spell," said Uncle. Silvia got up to help him. I watched him move off down the hallway. In order to make his way, he leaned against the wall. Step by step, he became smaller and smaller, until he reached the bedroom, opened the door, and went in without closing the door behind him.

"How do you feel?" Silvia asked me, running her hand through my hair.

"Uncle is tired," was all I could manage to get out.

Aunt Silvana had called us, telling us to go ahead and eat dinner. She was now stuck in Soriano Calabro, checking another new museum before the impending exhibition.

"This work she does keeps her out and about a lot," Uncle observed. He ate very little, a forkful of salad, a smidgen—*un pizzuddìcchio*—of tuna, no bread. He poured himself a glass of water with his right hand, set the bottle back down exactly where he'd picked it up, as if there was only one place on the table where the water could be, then he picked up the glass again with his right hand, drinking in small sips. Every movement he made oozed exhaustion.

"Do you want to rest a little?"

He'd slept practically the whole afternoon.

"You know, Daviduzzo, if what I have now had been another carcinoma, like the first one I had, today I wouldn't be here to greet you."

"But instead, here you are, ready to fight and lift weights. If you ask me, they'll invite you to participate in the next Olympics, Uncle!"

He gave a faint smile that, however, died immediately on his lips.

"I'm a little tired."

He insisted on getting up without help, headed off for his room, and lay down on the bed, fully dressed.

"Do you understand what he just told you?" Silvia asked me.

"He can feel his energy fading, but tomorrow, after the chemo, he's going to feel better."

"No, that's not what he told you."

I knew that she was about to ask the last question, the definitive one. It was just a matter of bracing myself to keep from collapsing onto the carpet.

"Why do you think your uncle is always telling you to hurry up and finish writing this book of yours?"

I took an enormous breath. I felt my shoulders heavy, my head heavy, my thoughts heavy.

I got up from the table.

"I understand," I said.

"Where are you going?"

"Out. I need to make a phone call."

———

Sicily was there, before me, a dark silhouette that bled off into the night. It glittered with dots of light, they looked like so many little fires, evidence that the island had been inhabited for millennia. Sciascia said that its coasts and open beaches suggest a first and fundamental element of Sicilian life and history: its insecurity.

"Ciao, Papà."

Silvia had offered me her interpretation of Beppe's words concerning the failure of a physician to listen. It's just like listening to the frightened plea of a child who wants his parents, or his elder brother, close to him, she had told me.

"I'm in Reggio, at Uncle's place."

Beppe was a physician, just like my father. Both of them knew lymphoma very well. It must be a nightmare to know exactly what's happening to your body during an illness. Understand the meaning of the cracks in the structure. Know in advance the speed of how the body will fall apart. Fully grasp the scope of the drift.

"He's tired, Papà. He's got his chemo tomorrow. He's pretty beat down."

My uncle, despite the fact that I'd denied it all this time, really was in danger of dying. And he knew it. My father was well aware of it, too. Their medical studies had kept both of them from lying to themselves.

In the silence between one word and the next, death had appeared like a solid, concrete landing site.

"Papà, you have to call Uncle, you need to call him more often, he needs you, he needs to hear your voice, he needs your presence."

Far away, the lights of Sicily trembled, like a cry for help that's afraid of getting lost in the folds of the night.

It was the winter of my shattered nerves.

The branches were succumbing to the wind of anguish as they tore away the leaves of words.

They crumpled, they shattered, they scattered into the distance.

The skeleton of my tree no longer had their voice.

The only remaining hope was the roots.

That they might be deeper than I myself believed.

That they might prove to be more solid than I deemed them to be.

More than that I could not do.

Underground lay my anchor of salvation.

I went in and abandoned myself to Silvia's embrace. I laid my head on her legs, letting myself drop onto the sofa. I closed my eyes while her hands ran over the lines of my face, back and forth, as if to learn their shape, so that she could reel them off from memory, available at her fingertips.

After a few minutes, Uncle Beppe appeared in the living room.

He seemed much more chipper.

"My brother called me!"

"Who do you mean, my father?"

"Yes!"

The time had come to act from the script.

"You're not serious."

"I swear it."

Right to the bitter end.

"No, Beppe, I don't believe it."

"Yes, that was Francesco on the phone."

He was radiant. He was so happy that he'd already started to count the days on his personal calendar till the next phone call.

"One to nothing, my favor!" he said, laughing and walking around the living room, leaning against walls and chairs, while I manifested my feigned disappointment with grimaces and Silvia, who'd already figured it all out, smiled, her eyes brimming over with tears.

THE DAY AFTER MY MEETING with the samurai, I got up before dawn, at a quarter to five. My flight was leaving at six twenty.

In the hushed darkness, you could barely hear the waves sucking back out, the sound was faint. Lampedusa seemed to have withdrawn into an elsewhere, far from the clamor of the mass media and the spotlights. There was a lovely, powerful silence.

All the liqueurs from the night before still stood on the table, from the limoncello to the wild fennel.

Melo walked into the kitchen. He'd risen early, as was his custom. Without a word, he automatically performed his usual morning actions: open the cabinet, get out the espresso pot, fill it with coffee, put it on the flame, lean against the cabinet, nod off, snap to at the gurgling of the espresso spewing into the pot.

He got out three cups, poured the espresso, and with a voice still slurred with sleep, asked if I wanted sugar.

"*Nonsi, amaro 'u pigghio.*" No, I take it bitter.

He sugared his own, then took the coffee to Paola in the bedroom. When he returned a few seconds later, he was wide awake. He had a prodigiously fast metabolism when it came to processing caffeine. He was hopping around the kitchen, he was washing dishes, he was whistling a song by Domenico Modugno with perfect pitch. His voice was clear and present.

"Your father was chief physician, wasn't he?"

"Yes, in cardiology."

He started to dry the utensils.

"And how did he behave with the doctors, the nurses?"

"He always stood up for them. As far as I can remember, that was one of the subjects of the very few arguments that Papà ever had at the dinner table with Mamma. Oh Lord, they weren't full-blown arguments, they were both in agreement. Now that I think about it, they were the longest monologues I ever heard out of my father in my whole life. Papà would talk about the exhaustion that inevitably builds up in a ward, both among the doctors and the nurses. And he would say that, unfortunately, the more the work load built up—and sometimes that load was really huge because they were understaffed for the number of patients they had—the greater the risk of a real mistake. It was the whole system, managed by corrupt and incompetent administrators, that put everyone into those conditions of risk, both the patients and the medical staff, physicians and nurses."

After putting the milk on the flame to heat up, Melo had started to gather the linen in from the line. It was dry but still faintly damp. The sea air is relentless.

"I'm just asking because I'm curious."

"About what?"

"About the fact that at your house you already had all the answers that you're trying to find here."

"What do you mean?"

Now that he'd taken it in, he started to fold the linen.

"It's not like the work your father did is all that different, the way I see it—generally speaking, I mean to say—from the work that the commander of the Capitaneria di Porto does, in other words, you see. That's probably at least in part why you're so fond of this whole story: The way I see it, there's a strong parallel between the Italian Coast Guard and the Guardia Medica, or emergency medical service."

Paola had just gotten up. She gave Melo a kiss, nodded a quick good morning to me, sat down at the table, and began her breakfast with a slice of apple pie she'd made the day before.

"There's no need for you to come take me to the airport, too, Paola."

"Melo isn't taking you," she mumbled.

"He isn't?" I asked.

"No, I don't like driving a car this early," Melo replied. He'd just finished folding the linen.

"I'm going out to take a picture of the dawn," he said. And he slipped out the door.

Paola had poured herself a mug of hot milk. She was sipping it, holding the oversized mug close to her face with both hands, as if it were the only source of warmth in life. Then she lit up her first cigarette of the day.

She spoke in a low voice.

"What's happening on Lampedusa, and what's been going on now for twenty-five years, is like a car crash that just keeps happening. There are survivors, dead victims, and the injured, and since I live in an apartment overlooking the street where the crash takes place, I have reporters who knock on my door and ask me questions. But it's the people who were in the car crash who really ought to be interviewed, they're the individuals we should be listening to. I just happen to live where I do, whereas they have gone through full-fledged adventures to get here. We can offer emergency first aid, cookies, bottled water, and hot tea, and we can do our very best to help them continue their journey. But instead, they, the true subjects of this story, the ones who ought to be listened to in order to better understand this mass exodus, they're just locked up in the Centers, and told to keep quiet when it comes to their rights and their motivations."

She poured herself a limoncello, put out the cigarette, and filled my glass, too.

"After all, it's still nighttime," she said.

We raised our glasses high and toasted in silence to something much bigger than any of us.

Someday an epic tale of Lampedusa will be born. Hundreds of thousands of people have transited through the island. Right now, what's still missing is a tile in the mosaic of this present day, and it is precisely the story of those who migrate. Our words are incapable of fully capturing their truth. We can name the border, the moment of the encounter, display the bodies of the living and the dead in our documentaries. Our words can tell of hands that provide care and hands that raise barbed wire fences. But it will be they themselves who tell the story of the migration, those who set out and, paying an unimaginable price, have landed on these shores. It will take many years. It's just a matter of time, but it will be they who explain to us the routes and the desires, who tell us the names of the people murdered in the desert by the human traffickers, the number of times a young girl was raped in twenty-four hours. They will explain to us the exact price of a life in those latitudes of the world. They will narrate to us, and to themselves, the story of the prison in Libya and the blows struck at every hour of the day and night, of the sudden sight of the sea after days of forced marching, and the silence that is forced upon them when the sirocco wind kicks up and there are five hundred of you on a sixty-five-foot fishing boat that has been taking on water for hours. It will be they who use the exact words to describe what it means to set foot on dry land, after escaping from war and poverty, pursuing the dream of a better life. And it will be they who explain to us what Europe has become and to show us, as in a mirror, who we ourselves have become.

You can't take a plane to escape from a war zone. You flee on foot and without a visa for the simple reason that visas aren't issued. When the land comes to an end, you board a boat. So let me start from the very beginning, which is a spring where we get the water we drink. After all, it's basically just the same story over and over. A Phoenician girl escapes from the city of Tyre, crossing the desert until she reaches the end of it, until her feet can no longer go on, because she has reached the sea. That is when she meets a white bull, which kneels down so she can climb onto its back, becoming a boat and plying across the waves, until it lets her off onto dry land on Crete. The girl is called Europa. That is our origin. We are children of a sea crossing by boat.

The shipwreck of October 3, 2013 took place before dawn, less than half a mile from the coasts of Lampedusa, on a line with the cove known as the Cala Tabaccara. The mechanics of the sinking were cruelly straightforward: At the sight of dry land someone, in order to make a light that could help to signal the location of the vessel, set fire to something, perhaps a blanket. There was diesel fuel everywhere aboard ship. Suddenly there was a blast of flame on the crowded deck. The packed crowd of passengers, afraid of being burned, instinctively recoiled to avoid the flame. That immediate stampede tipped the boat to one side, a decisive upset in an already quite precarious situation. The fishing boat overturned and in no time at all, sank to the bottom.

Between above and belowdecks, there were more than five hundred people.

The survivors numbered one hundred fifty-five.

Corpses recovered at sea: three hundred sixty-eight.

The tragedy of October 3 marked a watershed. For the first time, a vast number of corpses were seen, recovered, and counted on the shores of Europe. The pictures of lifeless bodies bobbing in the waves wound up on the screens of the mass media around the world. There was even a newborn fetus, still attached to its mother by umbilical cord. There was no sign of the vessel on the surface of the water, and yet corpses were scattered everywhere. In the hours that followed the first footage that appeared on TV, the world of Italian and European politics took the island by siege and lined up to appear on television.

A Sicilian proverb says: "*'U morto inzìgna a chiàncere.*" The dead man teaches you to cry.

"THAT DAY I was already at sea, we'd slept aboard the boat, the way you often did on summer evenings, both that year and the years before it. It didn't happen again in the years that followed. I didn't go out at night anymore after that. Not with my friends, not with other people, not alone. From that day on, my attitude toward the sea changed once and for all."

I'd met Vito at his home. At the center of the table, he'd set two glasses and a bottle of cold water just taken from the fridge. He'd taken the cork out of the bottle and poured the water, and then repositioned it exactly midway between him and me.

"I've always worked intensely, because I like to work. I started working when I was just a small boy, helping Papà in his woodshop. Then I became a programmer for automated production, back when computers were really big. The smallest one was about two hundred square feet. When I was done with my standard eight-hour workday as a programmer, I'd go back and help Papà in his woodshop, until in 1973 I quit my automated production job to devote myself full-time to the family woodshop. We would work for interior decorators and trade fair installations, which allowed me to travel the world. Then I came here to Lampedusa for the first time in 2000, for a break, to get away from work and the city. I was really tired. It only took two weeks of vacation here to fall in love with the place. Once I returned home, I decided to quit my job. I had an overwhelming drive to come back here."

Men of good faith, like my papà, maintain that, however inscrutable and mysterious the designs of the celestial spheres might be, it's nonetheless free will that serves as the needle of the scale, shaping the course of events. And if events are determined by the concatenation of actions and reactions, one linked to the other, in defiance of the undeniable mechanics of matter, then faith helps us to perceive the existence of something mysterious. We can call it intuition, we can call it illumination, or, to remain in an eschatological context, we can call it a vocation. It's inexplicable, but there are times you can detect the sensation of truly feeling something impalpable that calls to us through time, helping us—if not actually driving us—to embrace certain decisions, sometimes drastic ones, as if, on a hypothetical chessboard of reality, all the pieces were moving together, inexorably, in accordance with some invisible warp and weft, a plotline that ensured each individual piece would voluntarily make its move, culminating in the achievement of an exact alignment of space and time, so that a certain person would find themselves in a given place at a precise moment.

To save human lives that are drowning in the open sea, for instance.

"Only once all my employees had found another place to work—I've never liked leaving anyone without a livelihood—I shut down the woodshop and started living my own life in Lampedusa. I was fifty-two years old."

I looked at him through the bottle. Half of his body, the lower half, was distorted by the water. His shoulders, neck, and head, on the other hand, remained motionless. Vito stared at me and continued to do so until I drank the water he'd poured me.

"In 2007 they offered me a boat no longer in use, thirty-five feet long, that had once belonged to a fisherman. I decided to challenge myself and rebuild the boat from scratch. The next year I took the nautical exam and got my skipper's license. I rechristened the boat the *Gamar*, with the initials of my grandsons, the lights of my life. It used to have a completely different name, I'd changed it precisely because I'd radically modified the hull, turning it practically into another vessel. After the tragedy of October 3, a friend stopped me on the street. He said to me: '*O Vi*, do you remember the original name of your boat?' Of course I remember. The boat used to be called *Nuova Speranza*, the *New Hope*. It was true, this boat had given a new hope to all those that were rescued."

He reached out his hand and drank. He set the glass down and didn't look back at me again. His eyes were fixed on the facing wall, which was white and unadorned. The ideal surface against which to spot the invisible threads that weave our existence.

"Let me tell you about something that happened. I'm from Bari, I was a kid, I might have been thirteen, I was at the beach and I'd gone out on the water in a rubber dinghy, one of those round, ugly dinghies, without an engine, with Toni, a young man who was already an adult, I remember that because he had a driver's license and he was already driving a car. Before we headed out onto the open water, they'd warned us from the beach: '*Guagliò, statt accùrt, che sté vìnt sop a' terra!*'—Kids, take care, the wind is blowing from the land. When the wind blows from the land, it can be very dangerous. It pushes you out to sea. I was totally inexperienced, but Toni had said: 'Don't worry about the wind, we'll drop anchor.' And we went out in our rubber dinghy. The anchor consisted of a line tied to a large rock. When we were out in the open water, even though I'd already tossed the anchor overboard some time ago, I realized that, as the minutes ticked past, we were moving away from the land. 'Toni, we're moving out to sea!' I kept saying. 'Oh, don't worry about it,' he replied. I'm sure he knows, he's a grown-up, I thought to myself. So I calmed down. When it was time to head back to land, Toni told me to haul in the anchor so we could head in, and I pulled in the line but the so-called anchor simply wasn't there anymore: The knot had come untied and the rock was gone, who knows where, who knows how long ago. We were far, far out to sea. We tried to paddle, but it was no good, we weren't getting closer to the shore at all. Toni made a decision: 'I'm going to dive in with the line over my shoulder, and I'm going to start swimming.' He jumped into the water and I, without speaking, thought to myself: How on earth does he think he's going to be able to tow a dinghy like this? I tried paddling to help, but working together, our joint efforts produced no results whatsoever. In fact, if anything, we had drifted even farther out to sea. In the meantime, Toni had climbed back aboard the rubber dinghy. He'd started to feel sick, he was vomiting, he was suffering from stomach cramps, caused by exhaustion and agitation. I kept telling myself that it did no good to worry, the wind was blowing, that was true, but the sea was calm, and that was a huge help. I kept waving the towel to signal to the people on the shore that we needed help, convinced that sooner or later someone would spot us. But we just kept drifting farther away. The cars on land had become tiny. At a certain point, from the opposite direction, toward the horizon, I saw that a small dot was coming toward us, becoming bigger and bigger. I wonder if they'll see us, I kept thinking, I wonder if they'll see us. And, yes, they'd seen us, and how. It was a fishing boat. It was returning to the port of Palese. It veered toward us and from aboard the boat, a fisherman shouted to us: *'Guagliò, ma add'o cazz ve n'avìt 'a ji?'* Kids, where the fuck are you heading? They took us aboard, with our rubber dinghy, and we returned to land. It took us about an hour and forty-five minutes to reach the port."

Vito started staring at me again.

He poured more water and went on talking.

He'd found the thread.

Now he just needed to knot it back up.

———————

"The fishermen asked us to go to the Capitaneria di Porto to report the rescue. But Toni didn't want to, he went straight to get his car from where he'd parked it, leaving me there at the port to wait for him. I was inexperienced, I was young. Nowadays I would certainly have gone to the Capitaneria to declare: 'These gentlemen saved our lives,' because they sure had saved our lives, by bringing us in to port. Anything could have happened. This memory of the shipwreck came back to my mind a few days after October 3. It lit up in my head like a lightbulb. I said to myself: that's my story, from shipwreck victim to rescuer of shipwreck victims. It's a circle."

He lifted the glass and drank the water. He drank it with an insistent slowness, as if it were wine, as if to raise a toast, decades later, to the health of those rescuers of his childhood. He set down the glass, then he placed the bottle at the edge of the table.

There were no more obstacles between him and me.

"That night, the sea was calm and quiet. My friends and I took the boat out and stopped at Cala Tabaccara, to get something to eat and take a swim. We always went there. As usual, either we returned home very late, at two or three in the morning, or else we just waited until the next morning. We decided to spend the night at Tabaccara and then stay out so that the next day we could do some trawl fishing. We ate dinner and went to sleep. It was all quiet out, all dark, all normal. I was sleeping belowdecks, while my friends were up top, in the cockpit. I woke up because I heard the sound of the winch hauling up the anchor and then the engine being started. It must be dawn, I thought, it's time to go fishing. The boat had just started to move but after not even fifteen seconds, the engine stopped. I could also hear them talking up on deck. 'What could have happened? Something must be wrong with the engine,' was my conclusion. I got up immediately, rushing to the cockpit. 'What's happened? Problems with the engine?' I asked. 'No, no,' Alessandro replied. He was at the controls. '*Sento vuciàre*,' was his explanation. '*Vuciàre*,' as you know, refers to screams and laments. So he'd said, 'I hear people shouting, calling for help.' But neither I nor the others could hear anything. But out on the water there were lots and lots of seagulls and shearwaters. When they call they make a sound just like a human wailing or crying. 'Alessandro, it's just birds,' I said. '*No, no, no, io sento vuciàre, sento vuciàre.*' He insisted he could hear shouts of distress. He was so certain of it that I decided to go along with him. 'Alessandro, you can't see anything here, let's go out and get onto the water.' And so it was that he started the boat back up and we set out from the Tabaccara promontory. There were shearwaters flying in the air, there were seagulls. 'You see? You see?' Then I went to the prow of the boat to look out from there, ready to tell him again: 'You see that there's nothing out there at all?' Instead, I suddenly saw this strip of sea full of all these people shouting. They were crying 'Help!' All these dark silhouettes. All these arms. And that's when I thought: There's a tragedy going on. There were at least two hundred people. I immediately told my friends to alert the Capitaneria di Porto, it was out of the question to think we could rescue all these people, we needed help. Alessandro put out the call immediately. I have to tell you the truth: In those first few seconds, I was really afraid. How would we succeed in saving them all? There were already eight of us on the boat. How many more could we take on board? Two? Three? Not much more than that. Where would we even put them? That fear lasted about ten seconds, no more. I headed for the stern, I gathered life jackets and ropes. 'Alessandro, steer toward them.' And we started taking people aboard. They were miserable, naked, completely filthy with diesel fuel. When I managed to grab someone, they'd slide out of my grip. We managed to get three on board. My friends talked to them in English, but unfortunately I don't speak it, which is something I really regret. 'Ask them how many of them there are in the water.' And one of the young men we'd rescued answered: 'Five hundred sixty.' But there was nothing like five hundred sixty people on the surface. That was when I got my first certainty concerning the scope of the tragedy. We continued hauling in people. Without even counting them. Without thinking about it. Without the slightest idea of where we'd put them. Get one in and keep looking. Get another and move on. Another and move on. In the meantime, another little boat showed up, small, no longer than sixteen feet, lower to the water than mine. It was the *Nica*, Costantino's boat. I watched it out of the corner of my eye. Costantino was hauling these kids out of the water without even grabbing their hands, he was just picking them up by brute force, grabbing them by the seat of their pants and tossing them into the boat. He managed to get eleven into the boat. A trawler arrived. I thought: great, more help. Instead, as soon as they saw that we had all these people aboard, I heard a voice from the trawler: One of the two fishermen shouted to his brother: 'Fuck, steer that way, these bastards are throwing human beings overboard.' They'd mistaken us for people smugglers. They hadn't understood what was going on at all. An instant later, after they rounded the promontory, they, too, saw all those people in the water. They immediately started maneuvering to get as many of them on board as they could. That trawler had high sides, they were forced to throw lines overboard, hoping that anyone who was in the water would be able to get a solid grip, and then they could haul them up. There were some who were able, others who weren't. They rescued eighteen people. Around seven fifteen the ship arrived from the Capitaneria di Porto. They, too, started hauling in the people in the water, who kept shouting and sobbing. In the midst of tragedy, though, these people had a stroke of luck. That night a light sirocco wind had been blowing. And that sirocco had actually saved them, because it was pushing out of the southwest and toward the island. If instead of a sirocco, the wind had been a mistral, we wouldn't have been able to find anyone. The sirocco gave them the first, crucial element of help. We were the second piece of luck to come along. With my boat, we rescued forty-seven people from the sea, alive."

He poured himself more water. Only at the last minute did he notice that he'd filled the glass right up to the rim. The water was brimming over the top, ready to spill over. He set down the bottle and let a long, deep breath exhale from his chest.

"When I go to the port to check on the boat and I see all the scattered buoys in the sea, well: Dark buoys always give me a shock. I immediately think that it's people calling for help. Going back to the sea wasn't easy. It was ugly. We forced ourselves to do it, me and my friends. We told ourselves: Today we have to go out on the water. It had been a week. That first trip out was an ordeal. Your eyes don't rest in one place the way they used to. It was and it remains a gaze determined to find someone on the sea. Little by little, things have changed, but just a little, not entirely. Behind every wave, I continue to see people in the water."

The hand took the glass. As he raised it to his mouth, inevitably, the water spilled, in spite of the slowness of his gesture. The drops remained on the table, tiny puddles ready to evaporate into the muggy early afternoon air.

"I saw those young people again, you know? They call me Father Vito. They tell me: 'You are my father.' They're in my thoughts every single day. I suffer a little bit from claustrophobia and it always used to happen that, whenever I would board a plane, when they close the hatches and the plane wouldn't move, I'd get very upset and uneasy. I would feel terrible. Now, though, I just think of them right away. And then I have no trouble at all."

We sat there a while longer, as the song of the locusts invaded the room and the afternoon sun extended its dominion over the island.

COSTANTINO'S VOICE was faint, in contrast with the breadth of his hands. His life as a manual laborer could be summed up there, in those powerful fingers that have shattered stone. Fingers and hands were intertwined, motionless on the table, like tools laid down during a break from work.

―――――

"On that October 3 I'd gone out on the *Nica*, my little boat, *mia barcuzza*, along with my friend Onder. We had decided to get moving early, right after dawn, to beat the other fishermen to the punch so we could catch something for ourselves. We headed toward Rabbit Island. Suddenly we spotted a boat motionless in the water. It was Vito's boat. There were a huge number of people aboard. And right in front of our eyes we started to see bodies in the sea. They were almost all naked. Onder and I started trying to rescue them, but they'd slip out of our hands because they were covered with diesel oil. We'd grab them as hard as we could, but it was impossible to get a grip on their arms, on their hands, on their chest. The diesel made anything we tried to do impossible. Every effort failed. The first body that we managed to grab was by the belt around the waist, our hand grasped the belt and the next thing you knew, the boy's body was in the boat. Other boats that had come to aid in the rescues shouted: 'Forget about the dead, worry about the living.' We aimed at people wearing clothes, hauling them in by their trousers, their T-shirts, their belts. One body after the other. Grab the trousers, grab the cloth, there was no other way to do it. We'd recovered ten men, alive. We were moving our boat slowly, there was a very real danger of hitting some survivor with the hull of our boat. But all the bodies in the sea seemed to be dead. But during our very last circuit, before transferring the young men we'd managed to rescue to the patrol boat of the Italian Coast Guard, out of the corner of my eye I saw a young woman floating in the water move her hand. It was so hard to retrieve her. She was all covered with diesel fuel. She kept slipping away. But we finally managed to haul her in. I took off my T-shirt to dry her off, to clean the kerosene off her arms, out of her armpits, to cover her up. The young woman vomited diesel fuel, coughed, vomited again. But she was alive."

Costantino untied the knot of his fingers and opened his hands.

He sat in silence, staring at his own palms, as if they were a book, pages from a past that never stopped returning.

SIMONE HAD THE SKIN of someone who is always out on the sea: darkened, toughened by the sun, by the wind, by the salt air. His hair was long, with the color of a ship's cables. His beard was entirely white.

Paola and Melo's friend was waiting for me on the wharf of Cala Pisana, pacing twenty-five feet forward and then back. His wobbly gait seemed to replicate the bobbing of the boats. Simone needed to walk as he talked. That's a common condition among people of the sea: They're never at ease with the fixed nature of dry land. They need movement to regain their equilibrium.

"We Lampedusans have never done anything special, Davidù. It's normal, isn't it? You see someone in the water, you lean over from the deck of the boat and you do your best to grab him. Anyone who sees a person drowning does whatever he can to rescue him. It's not like we're heroes, after all."

Then my name changed in his phrasing. I became "A Dà."

"A," the vocative that invites one to listen, calling attention to itself. Followed by the truncated name, of which only the first syllable glitters, a sign of confidentiality and necessity, because what you want to communicate to the other person is urgent.

"*A Dà*, that morning I wasn't even planning to go out on the boat at all, but I'd woken up early, so I go out on the water at a quarter to eight. As I'm leaving the port I think to myself: to starboard or port? Let's go to port. And I almost immediately run into Vito's boat. It's loaded down with people. What on earth could be going on? I rev the engine to full RPMs, maybe I can get there in time and help out. I cross paths with the Italian Coast Guard and they wave for me to slow down, to go very slow. There has to be something in the water. I set the engine to dead slow and sail along, keeping a careful watch.

"And on the surface of the water I see a child's T-shirt.

A plastic bag.

An identity card bobbing on the surface.

A dead body.

A pair of shorts.

A pair of shoes.

A dead body.

Two slippers.

A bracelet.

Three dead bodies.

"*Mi vinni un arrivùgghiu nnu stomaco*...there was a sour taste in my stomach. I recover the first few bodies. They're all corpses. None of them are breathing. I grab others. They're dead, too. Each time I'm hoping that one of them will still be alive, but instead they're all dead. And then I see this tiny little thing, yea big, bobbing on the surface. A *picciriddo*. How old could that tiny child have been? A year? Two? He's not breathing either. *Mi si secca 'u cori.* It dries out my heart. I got there too late. This remorse obsesses me, not having been able to rescue anyone at all.

"In the afternoon the Italian Coast Guard asks me to help them locate the watercraft, they've identified a place where the fishing boat might have settled. I go back there and I dive. At that location, the seabed is about a hundred sixty-five feet down. I swim down and then suddenly, as if it were planned, I see a white patch open up beneath me on the seabed. It's sand. And right there, as if it had been set down from above, is the sunken refugee boat. It's an eighty-foot fishing boat, motionless in that white space. And all around, as if they'd been carefully placed on the sand, are the corpses. *A Dà*, I'm swimming and I'm crying. I swim and I cry. On the stern transom of the fishing boat, there are two bodies. They have their arms wrapped around each other. Both heads are turned upward, as if looking at the sky. I swim and I cry. I have to go into the hull to understand the situation belowdecks. I swim inside and everywhere I look there are corpses. One atop the other, in every space, in every nook and cranny. There are dead people everywhere. Corpses upon corpses upon corpses. Inside the fishing boat, there were two hundred fifty dead bodies. I didn't want to dive again as long as I lived, *a Dà*, I swear to you, I never wanted to go underwater again. If it hadn't been for customers who had already reserved and would be arriving a few days later, I would have stopped diving from then on."

Simone was chewing his lip.

His forehead was studded with drops of sweat, like punctures left by a crown of thorns.

THE CORPSES WERE RECOVERED and laid out in the hangar at the old airport. There was no other structure capable of holding them all. They covered a surface area stretching over a thousand square feet or so, one row after another, all in black body bags.

They were a dark constellation, on the southernmost church courtyard of Europe.

"There were all these coffins in a line, then two Eritrean *picciriddi*, one beside the other, beautiful, lying there on the ground, with nothing but a thermal blanket to separate them from the dirt. How can people do such a thing? Okay, I get it, we've run out of coffins, but how can someone leave dead little *picciriddi* on the ground? I went over to the policeman and *ci 'u rissi*, I asked him: 'What, are you not going to do anything?' So I went over and got a plank of wood, at least that way we could pick them up. They really were beautiful, those two *picciriddi*, they might have been at the most four years old. I thought about my daughters. I got a powerful knot in my stomach while I was laying them on the dais."

"Many corpses were unrecognizable, deformed by their prolonged underwater immersion, corroded by the salt, chewed at by the fish. The sea had invaded internal organs and tissues, some of the bones were shattered, the bodies were swollen to an unbelievable extent. In many cases, the flesh had broken and limbs had come off. There was none of the usual rigidity of death, and you couldn't recognize adults or children."

————

"They were people, but they looked like sponges."

"The mayor had asked us residents to offer help in taking in the relatives of the victims. News of the shipwreck had immediately prompted a vast international reaction and many relatives of the dead had come to Lampedusa. They almost all came from northern Europe. The arrival of the next of kin lasted a whole month. Many of them, the minute they got off the plane, collapsed in fits of tears. And what could we do about it? We embraced them."

"The first relatives to reach the island wandered around the hangar searching for anything—a particular mark, a ring, a bracelet, a necklace—that would help to identify them. But the bodies they were supposed to identify didn't even slightly resemble their memories or the photographic portraits that they'd brought with them. Petite young girls now had vast shapeless bodies. And there was often a part missing from the body that was to be identified: part of a leg, a few fingers, both eyes, the feet, a hand, the ears, an arm, the lower lip. There were bite marks everywhere."

————

"When the bodies were being identified, the heartbreak was inconsolable. When they weren't, same thing."

"A week after the tragedy, a container ship had tied up at the wharf to take the coffins to Sicily, where the bodies were buried, in no particular order. The Porto Nuovo was crowded with the victims' next of kin. The coffins had been transported from the hangar down to the wharf in refrigerator trucks, like so many loads of seafood. During the trip, the relatives had clambered onto the sides of the trucks, trying to lay flowers on the coffins—all of the caskets were black except for the ones containing children, which were small and white. The caskets were loaded onto the ship by a forklift which hoisted them high with its mechanical arm. On the wharfside, everyone was sobbing."

AT THE MOMENT that the refugee boat was overturning, I happened to be in Amsterdam doing a writer's residency. In August, my dearest friend Totò had died. A tumor in his colon had swept him away in less than fifty days. I'd watched as my friend withered, visible to the naked eye. Every time I went to see him, he weighed a few pounds less.

"How did he look to you?" Silvia had asked, seeing me return shaken from one of my last visits to the hospital.

"He seemed like a withered grape."

It was true, Totò seemed a dried-out petal. His fading not only struck me as unfair, it was really too fast, too unstoppable. I couldn't make sense of it. "Too" was the only word that I could use every time I thought of him, always in a negative connotation. Too close to death. Too distant from his normal self. Too sick to get better.

I stopped talking about Totò. With anyone. I avoided the topic. Life was abandoning my friend, unveiling his skeleton, and there was nothing I could do about it.

Totò had been the owner and the prime mover behind Altroquando, a shop that it would be far too little to call a comic book shop. The shop was on Corso Vittorio Emanuele II in Palermo, and it was a genuine cultural crucible. There were presentations and meetings with graphic novelists and comic book artists. It was a landmark in the fight for LGBT rights. When I lived in Palermo, for years I'd go out every morning and walk over to Altroquando. Totò would come out and we'd go get a nice espresso at the café, then we'd go back to the shop, I'd grab a random assortment of comic books, say goodbye to Totò, and then go home to read them. I'd take them back at lunchtime, keeping the ones I planned to buy, and then we'd go get lunch together in Ballarò or at the Capo. Life was good. At the end of June 2013, though, they found the tumor, and in August he died. A chasm opened in my chest. I shut myself up, closed off to the world. I wasn't capable of suturing the wound, because at the simple thought that Totò was gone, I felt like sobbing and sobbing, but I couldn't cry—my eyes would well up but I'd choke back those tears. All around me there was a safety net ready to catch me, but I remained stubbornly clinging to my pain because I could no longer see anything beyond my grief and sorrow.

The last time I went to see him in the hospital, two days before he died, Totò was completely high on morphine. He was smiling, he moved slowly, it was clear that he could no longer decipher reality. Instead, the visit before that, a week before his heart stopped, Totò told me a story.

The Buddha and one of his disciples were heading to the temple. At a crossroads, they chance to meet a woman. "Good morning," the Buddha greets her. The woman returns his greeting. The Buddha and his disciple continue on their way, and at sunset they reach the temple. When the Buddha goes to pray, the disciple addresses him. "Master," he says, "aren't you the one who preaches detachment from all things? So why did you greet the woman at the crossroads?" The Buddha replies: "Well, you see, I left the woman there; you're the one who carried her inside you." And he goes off to pray.

Those were the last lucid words that my friend spoke to me.

I had carried that inner malaise with me all the way to Amsterdam. I couldn't write a thing, and the world had offered me perfect excuses to pity myself.

Then the tragedy occurred off the coast of Lampedusa. Something clicked inside me. During my stay in Amsterdam, I had agreed to publish an online diary for the blog of the Nederlands Letterenfonds, the Dutch Foundation for Literature. On October 3, 2013, I wrote the following as it came to me:

> I walk along the canal, closely watched by the thousand-eyed houses of Amsterdam.
>
> The distant echo of the tragedy of Lampedusa has just reached me. The number of corpses that are still being recovered on the high seas is terribly great, and the final number refuses to be pinned down. It's a pitiless reckoning.
>
> The sky, as seen in the water, moves constantly. The bridge that cuts across the canal makes it possible to admire this paradox: things celestial tremble and things human remain solid. The banks of the canal, the glass of the windows, the irregular geometry of the houses leaning against each other like brothers who have just outfaced a challenge.
>
> Two lovers embrace in front of a boat in the gentle, warm air of this early October. The sky

*offers itself, a pure clear blue, and in the image that
the water reflects, the glints of light sparkle like
brief fireflies, quickly swallowed up by something too
serene and distant to grasp in full the anxieties and
joys of those who live on this side of life.*

*Here, in the heart of Europe, there is still a
strong memory of the severity of the sea. It's written
in the skin of the city, whose face is creased with
salty wrinkles.*

*Anyone who has had sailors among their neigh-
bors knows the rules.*

The sea breathes, while the sky does not.

*The sea gives and takes life, when it chooses to,
just like the sky.*

*Now the sea, the same sea that I have just
reached, accompanied by the canals, and which
bathes every coast of Europe, is full of dead bodies, migrants shipwrecked during this odyssey of
desperation.*

*Even the fish will go back to feeding on human
flesh.*

*A cat looks at me as two young people go by,
pedaling their bikes, hand in hand.*

*I am reminded of a poem by Ungaretti. The
context is completely different, and yet for me, now,
it speaks exactly of the soul of someone perishing
at sea, after trying to flee from poverty, separating
himself from life with this death in the water.*

Now the wind has fallen silent
And silent is the sea;
All is hushed; but I cry,
Alone, my heart's lament,
I cry of love, I cry of shame
For my heart that burns
Ever since I saw you and you gazed at me
And nothing but a helpless thing am I.

I cry out and my heart burns unceasing
Since I became
But a ravaged thing abandoned.

In the end, everything boiled down to these two simple truths: I'd never see Totò again, and the time we spent together had been a blessing. In the last page of my online diary, I finally faced up to that private grief.

A glimmer of light had begun to rip through the shadows of my anguish.

Silvia was holding my head, and I was holding on tight to her.

It had been little more than three weeks since October 3.

Dear Totò,
It's been such a long time since you told me about
the period you spent in Amsterdam. "It was 1971,"
you said while you were lighting your umpteenth
cigarette, "in Italy the Years of Lead were heating

up, the country was discovering heroin, and I was
a twenty-year-old kid disgusted with my country
and starving to get out and see the world." But
Amsterdam—the Amsterdam that I thought I'd
find in those words of yours—wasn't there in the
story you told: no crooked houses, no canals full of
geometric shapes, no paintings by Vermeer. Your
anecdotes were a celebration of how you hustled to
survive, a list of the thousand odd jobs you worked
and sofas you crashed on; they were evocative of the
flavor of cold beer and the tranquillity of a nice joint
smoked in a warm room; they were reminscences
of the eyes of your lovers, poor misfits, young men
on the loose just like you, except for one, a Cana-
dian in his fifties who was wealthy beyond anyone's
wildest imagination, and generous, too, who for a
while, when you returned to Italy, continued to send
you letters with money. Do you remember, Totò?
When you got to this part of the story, you always
acted out opening the first letter you got from him,
and you painted on your face the astonishment of
finding money in foreign currency, then you'd look
at me and burst out laughing, and once again you
had the eyes of a child, and they were gleaming gems
set in the creases of your face—the face of a Shake-
spearean king. But, I have to confess, my feelings
were a little hurt when, full of enthusiasm, I told
you that I, too, was going to go live in Amsterdam

*for a while, on a writers' residency, and all you had
to say to me was: "Then you can tell me what the
leaves are like, Davidù." I still couldn't understand
it, Totò, I hadn't devoted the proper attention to
certain aspects of the world, you were still alive, the
tumor had just been found, and even then I wasn't
ready for the idea that you might really die. I'm
not prepared for it even now, as far as that goes.
Every time I think about you, I still feel like crying.
I started pestering you with relentless questions
because I'd put together an infallible plan: "Where
did you stay? Is there a street, a square, a canal, a
coffee shop that you remember more than any of the
others? Maybe it still exists, and I'll go there, and
when I come back we can talk about it together."
I wanted to get to know your personal geography,
Totò, places I could photograph and then show you
when I got back. I thought it was a great plan, I
was convinced that it would work, "Look here how
it's all changed! And take a look at this, it's the
same as it was back then," maybe it would help to
alleviate your suffering. But life doesn't go along
with brilliant plans, it charts its own course without
taking advice from anyone, inscrutable as always.
Something moved faster than the calendar, I never
got a chance to show you the photos, and you left
this world before I even left for Amsterdam. That's
why I'm in Westerpark now, Totò. I bet anything*

that you came here, too, it's that long, long park,
you remember? Today there are people here rid-
ing bicycles, young people sunbathing, old people
strolling, people doing yoga, children playing, and
a tightrope walker trying to find the meaning of
life by standing balanced on a thread. Scattered
everywhere, trees. Their trunks are solid but not
too big, I can grasp my hands together when I put
my arms around them. The bark is both brown and
green, because it's covered with moss and, on brash
young branches, the leaves are changing color. I'm
only realizing it now, Totò: I've always gotten things
wrong when I think about the fall, it's not at all a
gray season, it's a symphony of colors that fade one
into another, in harmony. Green, sky blue, yellow,
yellow, brown, red, in all the different shades and
nuances, and the sky that ranges from white to
azure, and the thousand lights of the city that glitter
on the water and on the windowpanes. No season
has as many colors as autumn. And the leaves,
Totò, these leaves of Amsterdam are yellow, they're
green, they're red, and they tremble in the wind and
they dance for everyone, for the tightrope walker
and for the children, for the dogs trotting along, and
for me, for the old people, and for your eyes back
in 1971, when you were still twenty years old and
your beard wasn't white. And it would be so nice to
come back just to bring you a single leaf collected

*here, we'd laugh together because you'd have beaten
the cancer and I'd feel better, but instead, no, this
autumn filled with colors is going to end and winter
will come and rain will fall and it will be cold out,
and I'm just so afraid because the only verb that I'll
be able to use when referring to you will have to be
in the past tense, but here before me the leaves are
shivering in the wind, and now I know the answer
and, you know what, my friend?—it's a magnificent
October here in Amsterdam, the young people are
still in love, the beer is still cold, the houses are still
crooked, and the leaves, Totò, the leaves are yellow,
they're green, they're red, and they're so beautiful.*

IN THE LAST FEW MONTHS a number of things had
happened.

My father would often go to visit Uncle Beppe in Reggio, staying at his house for a couple of days. They'd go around to look at the archaeological sites where Aunt Silvana worked; they'd take pictures together and Uncle would send them to me on WhatsApp, accompanying them with messages of this sort: "Look who's come to see me." He was so proud that my father had traveled to visit him that I had no difficulty whatsoever imagining him with a broad grin when he sent me those messages. Sometimes he'd write "one to nothing, my favor." Sometimes, "Look at my brother sitting in my chair." Sometimes, "You're the only one missing." Uncle was also fighting against his shortage of white blood cells. On one occasion he'd been rushed to the hospital with a fever of over 102, and they kept him overnight under observation. They'd released him because the pharmaceuticals set him back on his feet. He slept badly at night, so he might nod off on the sofa at home, either in the morning or the afternoon. He'd started taking guitar lessons, even though he hadn't played in thirty years, and he often ran through the refrain of "Sei nell'anima" by Gianna Nannini. He'd asked me what my favorite Italian novels were, and then he'd bought the ones he still hadn't read. He'd especially liked *La vita agra* (*It's a Hard Life*) by Luciano Bianciardi and *Una questione privata* (*A Private Affair*), by Beppe Fenoglio. He'd also told me he was ready to reread his favorite novel in the world, Leonardo Sciascia's *Il consiglio d'Egitto* (*The Council of Egypt*).

Papà had learned to photograph people. He'd undertaken, in a fairly natural manner, the transition from inanimate object to live subject, in flesh and blood. It was as if the still life had been a necessary apprenticeship before he could properly approach a human being. The object had given him permission to reflect on his own intimacy and on the mystery of life itself.

"Rust might be, at first glance, a symbol of consumption, something that is beyond redemption," he had told me.

"But instead, something as useless as rust is capable of creating charming shapes that, taking form in space, suggest new perspectives."

In his close-up portraits, on the other hand, my father investigated the human being in the face of the enormity of existence. In his shots of faces, there was innocence, fear, and exhaustion. Papà had done a series of very powerful portraits from inside the hospital walls. Those were his latitudes, the places where he knew trajectories and areas of slack water like a familiar stream. He'd talked with his colleagues and become invisible, knowing perfectly well how to behave in order to respect the sterility of a room, the rights-of-way of staff as they moved in and out, the inviolable privacy of the patients.

"Compared to photographs of objects, with a person you have to capture an instant, and, in order to capture it, you have to anticipate its glow. This, like everything in life, is simpler if you try to do it with something that you know very well."

He'd started to call me on the phone, once every three weeks or so. That was already an immense improvement compared to the nothingness of the previous forty-two years. He told me especially about his visits to Uncle Beppe in Calabria.

"He gets tired easily. He took me to see a town in the interior that was entirely destroyed by the earthquake. I took some interesting shots, especially of the people standing guard around there. They had remarkably immobile faces. They seemed like so many rocks."

In doing portraits of faces, my father could sense the disintegration of life. The only reason his brother was still alive was medical therapy. And so, photography had become a tool and an objective, a question about the meaning of life and an answer to that question. In the final analysis, it was my father's way of trying to start a dialogue with God Himself, a dialogue that contained both an effort to understand and a conscious abandonment of self to the mystery of existence.

I CALLED PAPÀ on his cell phone.

I couldn't seem to get used to the idea that he might answer me away from his home.

The availability of a person had always been, to me, before the advent of cell phones, an unfortunate condition peculiar to physicians. And it was especially at home that a physician paid for his availability. "Today I'm available, on call," Mamma or Papà would tell us at lunch. Until the next day, the hospital would be able to reach out and claim them at any moment. The home phone could ring at any hour of the afternoon or night. The expectation-of-a-phone-call-that-might-never-come created a persistent condition of precariousness. My parents' work had followed them home, it sat down to meals with us in the dining room, it intruded into the bedroom. Those were special days, the days they were available, on call, when the phone line had to be kept clear, and the things my parents did were never wholehearted, fully experienced: Books were leafed through rather than read and music was used as a background for thoughts. I think that mentally they'd review the fastest route to get to the hospital by car. Sometimes the phone call alerting them to a greater or lesser medical emergency would come, other times it would not.

"Ciao, Papà."

"Ciao."

Cell phones have changed everything. Rescues at sea, to name one example. Those who set sail are diligently instructed: After a couple of hours they'll call such and such a number, the Italian Coast Guard will answer. Reading out the satellite coordinates on the smartphone, they'll communicate their position and await the ships hurrying to their aid. It's a mechanism that works, if the currents aren't too strong, if the waves aren't too high, if the rubber dinghies aren't taking on too much water.

"Are you at home?"

"No, I'm at Poggioreale, I'm photographing the ruins of the earthquake of Belice."

In the days before cell phones, when I was out of town or on a long trip, the only way to get in touch with my family was to use a phone booth, or worst case, a telephone in some bar in the mountains, with the periodic clicks from the phone company.

"How is it to photograph ruins?"

"So powerful. Even though it's only a few miles from the highway, the town has been deserted since 1968. Unfortunately, people prefer to ignore the screams of these places full of silence. Instead, those voices ought to be paid attention to and understood completely, because they constitute a real problem for all of us, and have done for many decades."

In order to be able to talk to people, you'd set an appointment, usually just before dinnertime, you'd put in the phone tokens, you'd talk to your family, that is, your mother, the indispensable contact: I'm alive, I'm eating, I'm washing, I've made new friends.

"Papà, will you come back to Lampedusa with me?"

"Certainly. When?"

It was necessary to create a precise fit between the person calling and the person receiving, both of them confirming their own presence in the place assigned to communication.

"We'd go back for the anniversary, October 3."

"That seems right to me."

The landline would create emotional cathedrals. Gripping the receiver of my home phone, I learned of the birth of my two youngest brothers and the death of my grandfather. In a phone booth that no longer exists, I whispered, "I love you," in another phone booth, I wept, in a third, I ran out of tokens before I had a chance to say, "I'm sorry, forgive me." There were phone booths that were considered, rightly, to be luckier than others.

"We'd go back and stay with Paola and Melo again, at Cala Pisana."

"Perfect. Let me know the exact dates, that way I can see Uncle Beppe before we go."

There existed a very precise cartography of emotions, a map that revealed a network of relations between the human being and the urban grid. Sometimes, there was a line outside the phone booth. That was often the case with the more popular ones. It often happened that you'd wind up discussing your personal problem with perfect strangers. It's easier to open up to someone you don't know. People would hammer things out, trying to get their ideas sorted before picking up the phone to say, "I miss you," "Farewell," "I need to touch you." Sometimes, while standing in line, twenty-minute flirtations would blossom, "It's your turn now," "It was a pleasure to speak with you," "Same goes for me," "Well, take care and good luck." Living in a place also meant compenetrating it with your own feelings, indulging in the luxury of consigning communication to the exact and irreproducible dovetailing of space and time.

ON A CLEAR DAY, during the flight from Palermo to Lampedusa, you can look down on Sicily from above. The interior of the island alternates arid, barren zones with luxuriant valleys. Water sources and springs, scattered over the territory, were one of the first tools of power—the distribution of water—that the Mafia used to take control of the region. After a few minutes in the air, while the aircraft heads north only to turn and set a course to the south, in the distance, seen from the mountains that surround it, my

Palermo stands there, lying open to the embrace of the sea and to its embrace of those who come from the sea, a city devoted to welcoming right from its very name, Πάνορμος, *Pan Hormos*, all port, a place of landings and departures. And then, behold the alternation of vineyards and farmland alongside ruins and rocks, until, without warning, white as a prayer, there spreads out over the remains of Gibellina, a town destroyed by the Belice earthquake, Alberto Burri's landscape artwork *Cretto*. Seen from that altitude, the *Cretto* is reminiscent of the sheets used to cover the dead. A filter, the white sheets spread over the corpse, in which respect and pity prove to be indivisible. The last stretch of the island that you can see is the long, long coastline, in which the sand, attacked from behind by the Mediterranean maquis, alternating with white limesone rocks, lords it over the land for mile after mile. Then, nothing but sea as far as the eye can take in. A few fishing boats, an oil tanker, a hydrofoil.

The extinct volcano with a small port at its feet is Linosa, then a further expanse of sea until you reach the barren, flat, black Lampedusa. The airplane drops lower and lower, giving the impression that it's about to land on the water. As soon as you step out of the aircraft, Lampedusa collapses on top of you. Light, salt air, and wind sweep over you, while the yearning to leap into the waves increases along with the desire to eat seafood as soon as possible.

"ON THOSE DAYS, I'm on strike, I don't want to talk about it, I don't talk to anybody, you can come visit me but it's as if I weren't here. Still, it's a good idea for you to come back, that way you can see what happens with your own eyes."

On the phone, Paola had been categorical.

"She never did get over October 3," Melo admitted, without embroidering the topic much. "She took it badly at the time, and every year she just tries to get through the day as quickly as she can."

We reached the bed and breakfast, we took possession of our respective rooms, and, seeing that the commemoration wouldn't be until tomorrow, we decided to take a look around.

"Shall we go see the Center, Papà?"

"*Amunì*," he replied in dialect. Let's go.

We crossed the town, lashed by a blazing sun. We climbed up onto the top of the rise, escorted by three stray dogs.

"Is the hole still there?" my father asked.

"Yes, back there, somewhere."

But he had already stopped listening to me. He was standing there, hands in his pockets and camera dangling from his neck, with no interest in taking pictures, his head somewhere far away. The geometric shapes of the Center, rigid and blocky, must have reminded him not of a prison, but rather the wards of a hospital. He was thinking about his brother, of that I was certain.

When Aunt Nunzia died, Papà asked me to come with him to the wake that was being held in her home in Capaci, where she had lived her whole life. I was nine years old. I barely even knew Aunt Nunzia, she was one of Grandma's sisters, and that family tie summed up her whole life as far as I was concerned. Stretched out on the bed, she seemed tiny under the white veil. Her arms were crossed on her chest, her hands curved over her heart, and there was a string of rosary beads intertwined in her bony fingers. She died an old maid. Next to the bed, sitting in chairs made of dark wood, Grandma and her sisters were weeping for her. "Poor Nunzia, *mischina*, poor little thing," they'd say, the syllables broken by their sighs. My grandfather was in the kitchen with the other men, all sitting around the white marble table. No one was saying a word. They were drinking espresso. The only sound to be heard: the tiny spoon stirring sugar in the demitasse cup, an action performed by all of them except my grandfather, who drank his coffee strictly bitter and black. My father must have learned it from him.

"Papà," I had asked him at some unspecified point in my childhood, I might have been four years old, "why does everyone drink their coffee with sugar and you don't?"

"I like the flavor of the coffee."

During that wake spent in the kitchen, I, too, was offered an espresso. I was a young man, by that point, nine years old, I was at a very respectable age. The offer of espresso unfolded in the most rigorous wordlessness, all it took was a glance from one of the men present toward an empty demitasse and a slight forward movement of my head and we understood each other. It was my grandfather who poured the coffee out of the espresso pot that was sitting at the center of the table. A gentleman—I have no idea who he was—handed me the sugar. I shook my head no repeatedly, even taking a couple of steps back. My grandfather reacted to my refusal by nodding with immense satisfaction. The beginning of a smile had even appeared at the corners of his mouth. He must have been quite proud of me if he'd allowed that symptom of happiness to glimmer in that severe framework of grief. After I drank the coffee, the schism of the world between "silent men in the kitchen" and "weeping women around the dead woman" was stitched back together by none other than me and Papà. We entered the room of the wake and we stood for a while before Nunzia's dead body, in religious silence. Perhaps I mentally recited an Ave Maria and a Salve Regina, I can't exactly remember. We said farewell to Grandma with two kisses, one on each cheek, I shook hands with all the old women in the room, we went back into the kitchen, we bid everyone present farewell with an almost imperceptible nod of the head and Grandpa put his hand on my cheek, patting my face, with a long and profound caress.

On the way back Papà suddenly started talking.

"Did you see Aunt Nunzia? She was so small in that bed. She was such a gentle person, always so kind."

Hands on the steering wheel, eyes fixed on the asphalt. He was entirely focused on what was in front of him.

"She'd never studied, she never went to school, she barely learned to read and yet she had a refined intelligence after her fashion, she never said a word out of place, her judgments were very carefully calibrated."

Who was Papà talking to during that drive home on the highway? Because I felt sure that it wasn't me that he was addressing.

"You might say that Aunt Nunzia lived a frugal life, and yet deep inside she nurtured a great treasure. You can't sum up a person by the books that they've read. She was a tiny creature, small and petite, but she was so very dear to me."

Maybe the car was the only place where Papà spoke in a loud voice. At home there must have been too much constant ruckus, with me and my brother always shouting. At the hospital, it must have been impossible to succeed in cutting out a moment and a space for himself. Instead, inside the car, with his arm stuck out the window, Papà had found the ideal place to evaluate, analyze, and ponder. The car must have become his secret hermitage.

I felt lucky to be there.

"There is a series of questions, each of them linked to the others, concerning the very meaning of life, among other things. Where should you look for it? In your work, in your studies, in some manual pursuit, in faith? Aunt Nunzia wasn't married, she never had children, and yet she never seemed unhappy. She emanated such a feeling of calm, such serenity."

That day, the inevitability of mourning showed itself to him for what it really was: the only certainty of existence.

"There's more richness in a single human being than in all the books in the world," he concluded after a long silence. Papà didn't speak again for the rest of the day. I think that he had somehow decided to kneel down, having set aside all pride, before the inscrutable mystery of life and life's hand-maiden, death. He stared straight ahead at the road before him, and clutched the wheel with both hands, as if it were the only handhold remaining to keep him from tumbling into the abyss.

BEFORE DINNER on the evening of October 2, I left Papà to chat with Melo in the dining room and I called Uncle Beppe.

"It was a fucked-up event."

That's how he began, with that dirty word he never used, and which revealed the full extent of the terror he'd experienced.

"I'm fine now, Daviduzzo, but yesterday they took me back to the hospital because I had a fever, a temperature of over 102. The second time in twenty days. But today I feel better and now I don't give a damn."

Like little kids, I thought, my uncle is using dirty words to make himself feel stronger.

"I'll tell you something funny, it's about circles and how they close. Do you know what the numbers 31 and 47 correspond to in the *smorfia*?" He was referring to the Neapolitan book of numbers, used to transform dreams into winning lottery bets. "My grandmother Giovanna—and this is one of the very few memories I have of her—the few times that she came to Palermo would send me out to bet on the lottery numbers. She always dreamed of the dead man talking, number 47, and she'd play it along with number 31. I have a very clear memory of having played that pair of numbers for a couple of times at the lottery stands. They were small sums, just a few lire. Once or twice, when I was an adult, I playfully bet on that pair of numbers. And yesterday, during the rescue, you know what happened? They brought the newspaper to me in bed. It's a very rare thing that my eye strays to the column with the lottery drawings. But yesterday, that was the very first thing I read. I was convinced I had to be hallucinating. I checked it again today, just to be certain. The Palermo drawing had first and second numbers of 47 and 31. My grandma must have sensed that I was in the hospital! And no one believes me!"

He burst out laughing. I listened to the full extent of his laughter. It was hale and robust, and it gave a glimpse of what deep well of despair he'd risen out of. Only when the laughter died out did I speak to him.

"Did you tell Papà that you had to go to the hospital?"

"No, no, don't tell him, it will only worry him. Why don't the two of you just enjoy Lampedusa. Anyway, I'm going to fucking kick this lymphoma, and its bitch of a lymphoma mother. Big hug to you."

Maybe he'd gotten tired. Maybe it was the thought of my father being upset that had shaken him. The fear had re-emerged in the syllables he uttered. If there was one person my uncle was terrified at the thought of being separated from, that was my father. Their love was woven of continual distant gazes, like the vintner and the vineyard, who understand and love each other from afar, coming into contact only at the time of the harvest. It was a sentiment embroidered by each of them remaining in his own room, from which perch, with the opening of the smallest breach, the eye confirmed the presence of the other, and that presence alone filled the heart.

"All right, then. Ciao, Beppuzzo."

"Daviduzzo, hold on, there's one last thing I want to tell you, another thing about how circles close."

And I listened to him, holding everything in deep inside, as the shivers ran up my back and my right foot tapped out a rhythm on the sand of Cala Pisana.

The next day, Papà and I left the B&B bright and early.

"So, Paola, are we agreed that we're going to meet up later?"

She must have woken up a fair bit before dawn. Most likely, she hadn't slept at all. She responded with a nod of the head, which could have meant anything or nothing at all. She was smoking and looking out to sea, like someone who's lost a close friend and, not finding any other way out on the anniversary of that death, gives herself up body and soul to the torment of memory, waiting until the calendar can establish a new distance between her and her grief.

It was a hot day, it must have been eighty-five degrees or so.

"Maybe we can take a swim later," my father had said.

"Maybe so," I'd replied.

There were many commemorations of the October 3 tragedy, none of them connected to the others. Every association—though you might go so far as to say every private individual—observed its own commemoration, in a powerful atomization of memory, a broader mirror of the fragmentation that's in the air across the island. A march had been organized by one association, an interreligious observance in church by another association, a procession of government and European authorities had been invited by the military. The island teemed with television news cameras and journalists, all ready to leave the following day, when the summer season would officially be at an end and Lampedusa would once again empty out until the following summer. Papà spent a solid half hour photographing dogs sleeping in the shade of benches to shield themselves from the hot early morning sunshine. He'd scratch their backs. Eleven months had passed, but he'd returned, as promised.

We noticed lots of fishing boats coming back into port.

"Che succirìu?" we asked at the wharf. What's going on?

"Innìeru alla Tabaccara a ricordare." They'd gone to Tabaccara to commemorate.

They were a regular flotilla. They'd opted for a small, private observation, far from the spotlights and commotion of the mass media. After tying up, many of the fishermen crossed themselves, kissed their right forefingers, sent the kiss off with quick glances toward Cala Tabaccara, and then said farewell to each other.

A number of survivors walked through the streets of the town, returned especially for the commemoration. Bewildered by the presence of all those video cameras, they moved in groups, side by side, like a phalanx. "Poor creatures," was the first thought of one old man as he saw the way they moved in compact formations. "All they want is a grave to be able to mourn, a headstone before which they can pray for the relatives and friends they saw die before their very eyes. Still today, there are no graves bearing those names. They aren't asking for anything more. But what do we give them instead? No answer and the TV cameras of the national news at lunch time, stuck right in their faces."

We went by the barracks of the Italian Coast Guard. It was definitely a short visit, not even the time to drink an espresso with the commander.

"What kind of work do you do, sir?" the commander asked my father, as they were shaking hands.

"Cardiologist, retired now."

"So you know something about emergency situations."

215

"I understand you perfectly."

I saw a gleam in both their eyes, a sort of tacit pact whereby they would add nothing more in the presence of someone like me, who did not belong to that special brotherhood of those who touch death directly on a daily basis.

A moment later, the commander's telephone started ringing.

"Could you excuse me for a moment?"

The call was coming in from a patrol boat out on a mission. A couple of hours ago, they had recovered more than five hundred people, and, while they were bringing them to a Navy ship to transfer them, they had intercepted a rubber dinghy with a hundred fifty-four young people aboard.

"What kind of conditions are they in? Very bad shape? All right then, let's see."

The commander gave absolutely no signs of anxiety. That must have been his way of transmitting an air of confidence.

"How are you all? Everyone's okay? So, okay, go ahead and proceed with the recovery, and we'll talk when the operation is complete."

He looked up at us, the phone clamped between shoulder and neck, holding both arms out as if to apologize. We said goodbye with a quick bob of the head.

"It never ends," Papà blurted out, descending the stairs of the barracks. And he said it as the doctor that he was, as if he'd put his lab coat back on and the world was a patient to be treated. He stopped to look out over the sea. He stood

there, measuring himself against the vastness of that expanse of salt water. If we'd been in the car, he'd probably
have expressed aloud the maelstrom of thoughts that was
flowing through him.

He seemed solid on his feet, but it was pure appearance.

"Let me take you to a place, Papà, let's hope it's open."

He followed me without asking questions, making an
effort to keep up with me.

In the summer, when I was small, me, Papà, and my little
brother would go out into Nature. Nature was a trail through
the woods that ran from close to my maternal grandparents'
little house in San Martino delle Scale, all the way up to the
main square in town. In Nature, overhead there dominated
the twisted braiding of the tree branches, on the ground was
a carpet of rotting leaves, and alongside, as your traveling
companion, there ran a small brook. The whole hike was full
of the happy sound of running water, the babbling brook.
Light filtered down through the branches, creating a dra-
matic chiaroscuro effect. I walked along, bouncing from one
brightly lit patch to the next, as if that were the only way to
keep from getting lost in the woods. If I was running too
fast, I'd turn around suddenly. Papà would be there, holding my little brother by the hand, his eyes focused on me.
When we got to the town piazza, Papà would buy the newspaper and read it, sitting at the bar, sipping an espresso. My
brother would eat a Cono Palla, a crunchy ice cream cone,

and I'd play video games, especially Frogger. We'd return
home along the same path. On one of our first excursions
out into Nature, Papà found a walking stick as tall as he was.
The club of power, he called it. He took it with him wherever
he went, he'd lean on it when we stopped to rest, and he used
it to determine the pace of our walks. To me, power meant
being able to perform these acts: to guide others along a
path, keep an eye on those hiking, dictating the pace they
walked at and when they stopped. The only reason I wanted
to grow up was to inherit that stick. I wanted to grow up so
I would be strong enough to hold it with just one hand, just
like him. Back then my father struck me as a man in full, but
he was just a young man, an overgrown kid.

We walked down the steps of a very narrow lane, or *vicolo*,
where the thirteen-year-olds of Lampedusa held hands,
swearing undying love.

"We're going to Porto M., an attempt to bear witness to
what is happening. Over the years, the young people of the
Askavusa collective of Lampedusa have gathered a number
of objects that were left behind in the vessels that landed on
the island. The first ones arrived here in the nineties. Because no one knew what to do with them, they were all piled
up in the open space next to the Porto Nuovo, one atop the
other. Before long, the open space had become a full-fledged
refugee boat graveyard. Once it was full to overflowing, they
took them away. Now there are only four of them left in the

open space. Right there, you see them? They look like an oversight, something forgotten, rather than the result of an unfinished clean-up project."

I told him about Franco, the island's carpenter, who in 2009 was a witness to an invisible tragedy.

"A refugee boat had landed, recovered in the open sea by the Italian Coast Guard. When the people landed, everyone was surprised by the way that those who had landed just stayed there, on the Molo Favaloro, staring at the horizon. They were waiting for a sister boat. Those two boats had set sail together. Their brothers and sisters were on the other refugee boat, their children and their parents, their friends and their comrades from the prison. That second refugee boat never landed. There must have been four hundred people aboard. It happened two days after the earthquake in L'Aquila. There was very little discussion of it. In the absence of dead bodies, the news doesn't really exist. And yet for those who were there on the wharf, it was a brutal blow. It upset Franco more than anything else that had ever happened to him. As he was walking, he noticed among the wreckage of a refugee boat two planks lying one atop the other. They looked like a crucifix. Franco is religious and the cross is a symbol with deep meaning for him. And so he decided to build crosses out of the planks from the refugee boats that landed on Lampedusa, and then give them to as many people as he could. It was his way of awakening people to this situation."

Papà looked out over the open area where for years the cemetery of the refugee boats had existed.

"Just think the kinds of things those wooden planks must have seen," he murmured. His voice was faint, a whisper that had escaped from the stream of his thoughts.

"One of Franco's crosses was acquired by the British Museum. Images referring to Lampedusa have proliferated and are spread everywhere. After that phantom tragedy, Franco had worked with several of his friends to restore a warehouse, setting up a shower in it, to practice a sort of work of charity, but *ammucciùni ammucciùni*—without fanfare. He'd take the young men who'd wormed their way out of the hole in the fence around the Center so they could get cleaned up, and give them fresh clothing: socks, T-shirts, underwear, sweaters. Little by little, even some of those who regularly inveighed against these immigrant kids started leaving bags in front of the warehouse with donations of shampoo, soap, shoes, and trousers. They were seeing people on the street who were malnourished, barefoot, raggedy, and so they did their best to help them with their primary needs."

We'd reached Porto M.

"It's open, let's go in."

The objects displayed on the walls, set on the shelves and consoles, immediately imposed themselves above and beyond all other thoughts.

"It looks like a museum," Papà whispered. He observed the objects, and he must have put them into perspective immediately, because they were telling him the unfiltered story of the lives of those who had undertaken the journey.

The way they had left. What they had brought with them. What they considered indispensable. What you choose as your traveling companion as you set out on this adventure.

He started to take pictures. The camera lens as an extension of the diagnostic eye. My father moved like a physician.

These were the objects found in the refugee boats: tennis shoes, rubber sandals, canteens, plastic bottles, canvas carry bags, porcelain mugs, glass jars, drinking glasses, a bottle of almond milk, a carton of ordinary milk, packets of sugar, boxes of fruit juice, plastic food containers, cans of carbonated beverages, single-serving packets of jam, cigarette packs, bags of tobacco, lighters, maps, medicine, tablets, suppositories, ointments, pills, sprays, medicine dispensers, toothbrushes, toothpaste tubes, combs, toiletry bags, barrettes, skin creams, lipstick, chapstick, razors, insect repellents, shoulder bags, jars of spicy sauce, bottles of olive oil, jars of preserved tomatoes, a ketchup bottle, bottles of milk, a can of Coca-Cola, a can of bitter soda, a can of tuna, a pack of moist towelettes, packets of spaghetti, apple juice, tea bags, jars of preserved vegetables and fruit, cooking pots, lids, glass plates, colanders, teapots, coffee pots, portable camp stoves, pliers, knives, padlocks, screwdrivers, keys, shears, cell phones, little black dresses, women's dresses in solid navy blue, flower-pattern dresses, jeans, scarves, a beach wrap, T-shirts, wallets, rings, tape cassettes, CDs, copies of the Bible and the Koran, prayer books, rudimentary fishing poles and equipment.

I was walking and he was trailing after me, thirty or so feet behind me. When I couldn't see him anymore, I'd stop. I knew that he was examining something through his lens. A silhouette, a crumbling wall, a padlock that hadn't been opened in years. The sun was high in the sky. It was ten in the morning, it was hot out, and the sea looked like something out of a fairy tale. Papà must have taken a satisfactory number of shots, and in fact he had quickened his pace. When he caught up with me he asked: "Where are we going?"

"To the cemetery."

It was located at Cala Pisana, on the highest ridge above the inlet.

We had come back to our point of departure.

Outside the front gate we met Paola.

As the crow flies, less than two hundred yards separate the cemetery from Paola's home.

"Do you know that she was in charge of composing the inscriptions on the graves of all those who died at sea?"

"Really?"

Paola tried to downplay it, but the scope of my father's astonishment must have been sufficiently large to soften her stubborn determination to accept praise, persuading her to reply.

"At first, there was nothing written at all, just the dates carved into the cement. Working with an association I belonged to at the time, we sent a letter to the old mayor, telling him that we intended to improve the graves, putting a proper commemoration on each headstone. The mayor, at first forbade us from doing so, but then he did it himself in person. They put plaques on each grave that read: 'unidentified immigrant, of the male sex, of African ethnic origin, black in color.'"

"Was that really what they'd written on the graves?"

Paola lit herself a cigarette.

"Yes, that's what the signs said, and in fact all holy hell broke loose. The mayor defended himself, saying that he'd just copied what was written on the medical examiner's reports. Then it was the new mayor who personally gave me the job of replacing the old inscriptions with new, more decent ones. I spent days and days looking at a blank sheet of paper. I defy anyone to figure out what to write about dead people you've never met in your life. When I thought it over carefully, though, it dawned on me that the only information I could put down had to do with the circumstances of the recovery of the bodies and the details of their death. The first one was Ester Ada, a young woman who died during the open-sea rescue. The exact circumstances of her death were never entirely clarified. More than a hundred young people were rescued by the *Pinar*, a Turkish freighter. Our government at the time, though, refused to give the freighter authorization to enter Italian territorial waters, and so the *Pinar* remained in the open seas for five days with Ester's corpse on board. After five days, permission was finally given and the freighter docked at Lampedusa, landing the young people and Ester's dead body."

Paola had started to walk toward the cemetery.

"A religious rite was celebrated, with the enthusiastic participation of the island's residents, especially the women of Lampedusa."

She had started to walk more quickly. We turned into a small side walkway, and a short distance later Paola's feet came to a halt.

"And here we have Ester."

The inscription read: *On 16 April 2009, the Turkish freighter* Pinar *on course for Tunisia came to the aid of a vessel in difficulty. In spite of forbidding conditions on the sea, the crew of the freighter managed to rescue 155 migrants, all of sub-Saharan origin, bringing them all aboard the freighter. Also, the lifeless body of Ester Ada, age 18, Nigerian, was brought aboard the freighter. For four interminable days, the* Pinar *remained 25 miles to the south of Lampedusa, blocked by an absurd stalemate between the governments of Malta and Italy, which both refused to allow the freighter to land. It was not until 20 April that the ship was authorized to enter Italian territorial waters. The migrants were finally welcomed to Lampedusa.*

There was no wind that morning, and yet Paola was shivering. She sniffed loudly and then spoke without looking at me. It was as if her remaining strength had been focused on uttering that phrase.

"Talk to him."

And she pointed to an elderly gentleman with a watering can in his hand, who was heading toward a grave. Then she started for the exit, only to stop a dozen or so paces away.

"Will you be there for lunch?"

Having lost her bearings, she needed a purpose.

"Yes, of course."

She still didn't budge.

I asked her: "Why don't you make a nice pasta with swordfish and fried eggplant? It's so good the way you make it."

Paola had started to nod her head.

"And make sure you add some nice fresh calamint."

Paola lifted her right hand, as if to say, "Yes, that's right," nodded again, and started walking toward home, limping with every step.

The inscriptions on the graves weren't definitive. There was no way they could be. They reported all that was known: the gender of the person buried there. After that was a succession of indeterminate statements.

OF PROBABLE SUB-SAHARAN ORIGIN.

AGE SOMEWHERE BETWEEN 20 AND 30.

AGE SOMEWHERE BETWEEN 30 AND 40. Following that, the date of recovery of the body, which often did not coincide with the actual date of death.

The name, the country of origin, and the age remain unknown.

The gentleman who Paola had pointed out was waiting for us. They'd spoken on the phone. His name was Vincenzo and from 1978 until 2007 he'd been simultaneously the custodian, in charge of recovering the dead, and the entire and sole staff of the mortuary, responsible for sealing caskets and digging graves, as well as the attendant, the mason, and the gardener of Lampedusa's cemetery.

He told us about the first boat to come in from the sea that he tended to personally.

"They were all dead. The current had driven the boat in close to the port. It was 1996."

The military authorities summoned him because the stench of rotting corpses was so strong that no one had managed to get close to the refugee boat. In order to recover those corpses, Vincenzo needed to run over to his house. There he got a mint bush that he kept on his balcony and, carrying it under his arm, he headed back to the port. He tore off a few mint leaves, rolled them up, and stuck them up his nostrils. They weren't enough. The stench was still far too strong. So he bought a face mask at the pharmacy and stuffed it full of mint leaves. Only then did he manage to get close to the corpses. There were twelve of them. Vincenzo took them to the mortuary at the cemetery, and there he cleaned them one at a time.

"Over the years, I've buried more than eighty people who died while crossing the Mediterranean."

Vincenzo really had built the cemetery with his own bare hands. He had planted the trees, built the walls, created the walkways, and found the space to bury those who had arrived from the sea. He continued to return to the cemetery every day, on foot, health allowing. He swept away the leaves, cleaned the walkways, watered the plants. Since he'd retired, there was no one to do those chores. The water that he brought in his watering can served that purpose, to prolong the care for the dead, even for the dead he had never met.

Those first twelve corpses were buried in a space that Vincenzo had created at the center of the cemetery. They were eleven men and a woman. The men were arranged along a horizontal row, one beside the other. Then the time came to bury the young woman. The patch of land available was what it was, and so Vincenzo, in order to give the young woman the privacy she deserved, planted an oleander and buried her behind it, so that the leaves and the shade would protect her from everything, from the sun and the winter, from the mistral wind and from unfriendly glares. For every grave, he built a wooden cross. In the years that followed, there was a controversy because some people felt that some of the dead were Muslims and the cross was therefore not a suitable symbol for them.

"To me, no human being is any different from the others. This is how we treat people here. We bury them in the earth, in the shade of the cross, because we're all equal. We could be black, or green, or red, but inside we all have white bones."

Vincenzo had started walking again, one small step after another. When he came even with a row of crosses, he watered the plants, swept away leaves, swept the marble, changed the flowers. Once he was done, he headed toward the exit, turned around one last time, and waved goodbye to us.

I WAS FOUR YEARS OLD. We were at Marina di Tusa. On the beach there was no sand, only rounded stones, and so when you entered the water you had to walk with both arms outstretched to keep your balance, then, as soon as your feet touched the water, you'd dive in, because the beach dropped straight down without warning. Papà had taken me with him and then, putting both arms under my armpits, he had stared into my eyes with great seriousness.

"Ready?"

I had no idea what he was talking about.

"Yes," I replied. It was always the right answer if you wanted to win him over, whenever he suggested anything.

"Shall we go watch a shoot-'em-up at the movie theater?"

"Shall we spend some time in Nature?"

"You want to come with me to the station to pick up Uncle Beppe?"

Yes, Papà.

Anything you ask.

The sea came up to his chest. The fine gold chain with Jesus Christ on the cross looked like a fish swimming around his neck. I couldn't touch bottom and I felt Papà's warm hands under my armpits. Then he smiled at me.

"So, are you ready?"

"Yes."

And he tossed me as far as he could, out to sea, where the water was dark blue and not even his feet could touch bottom.

I started striking out furiously with my arms. But then I saw that Papà was relaxed. Now I understand that he must have been experiencing a terrible state of internal conflict, torn between the urgent need to come get me and waiting to see how I'd do on my own, with the risk of my going under and getting a bellyful of water. But he managed to stay still and just kept watching me. That could only mean one thing: that my father trusted me. My furious thrashing grew less and less chaotic, and my arms started alternating strokes as my legs kicked. It had happened. I was staying on the surface, just like him. I could feel the shivers running down my spine and the pride bursting in my chest. I knew how to swim. My father had made a bet on me, and I hadn't disappointed him.

I spent the rest of the summer in the water. I learned freestyle swimming and how to freedive.

In my early childhood, it was easier to talk to my father.

"How do you move your feet?"

"Like this."

"What if I get tired?"

"Just do the dead man's float and turn your head to breathe."

"What if there's a riptide?"

"You don't even go into the water."

"And what if I see an octopus go by?"

"You stay still and watch it, then when it swims close to you, you reach out fast and grab it."

We were discovering life: I'd call things by their name for the first time and he'd try and explain them to me. "Why is the sun hot? Does the sea think? If someone dies, do they dream?"

We swam together, stroke by stroke, turning our heads to breathe, once on the right, then on the left, feet moving at a steady rhythm, abdominal muscles clenched tight, tummy tucked in. I would align my course to match his, following his trajectories, he was much faster than I was, but the wake he left was clear and I felt happy to swim after him, because that way I had a direction to follow while I was learning to use the sea as a warm blanket, capable in the future of warming my heart during the winter of my life.

––––––––

PAOLA WAS SITTING at the table. She'd lit herself a cigarette while another one, forgotten, was burning away in the ashtray.

She was devoured by ghosts.

Melo was a spectacle of restlessness. Sitting on the sofa, he obsessively checked the monitor of the security camera focused on the front door of the house, as he leafed through a book that, after scant seconds, he'd shut again, then he'd get to his feet, pick up another book, shoot a glance at the monitor, sit back down, leaf through the book again for a few seconds, shut the book, glance at the monitor, get back to his feet, and pace the room. He spent a good fifteen minutes like that. Papà, sitting out on the veranda, was editing his photos on the screen of his camera. Suddenly, Melo leapt to his feet. On the monitor of the security camera, he'd glimpsed a tiny point that was walking toward the house. He crossed the patio barefoot and went to open the front door.

"Paola, Simone's here!"

Her friend's name seemed to stir her from that torpor.

"What are you doing here?"

It was eleven thirty and it was ninety degrees out.

"Melo invited me to come to lunch, and then I wanted to say hello to Davide and his Papà."

Paola started to reply. She gesticulated with her hands, but no words emerged from her mouth.

Simone sat down at the table.

Melo pretended to be uninterested, but it was clear that all his attention was focused there.

"*A Pà,*" Simone began, addressing Paola in abbreviated form. Then he remained in silence. Only when Paola turned around to look at him did Simone continue talking.

"It's done. I did it."

"When?" asked Paola, furrowing her brow, leaning toward her friend.

"Just now. I tied up not ten minutes ago. I didn't even take a shower."

Paola opened a pack of cigarettes. The time had come to resume smoking consciously.

"Tell me about it," she said, once again concentrating on the present.

Melo let a smile appear on his lips, then he stretched out, grabbed a book, and pretended to read it.

Simone told her that he had been contacted by a television journalist.

"They wanted to do a piece on October 3. *A Pà,* they asked me to take their scuba diver out for underwater filming. And you know where? Tabaccara."

In extreme situations, men are not at all as books describe them.

"I hadn't dived since then."

It's unclear whether their actions will amount to a small apocalypse or a foundational act.

"So I replied without thinking. 'All right, let's make this dive,' I told them. I went under out there two hours ago, Pà."

Simone had described to me what he liked so much about the sea.

"The silence. And the music that you hear inside you when you look at the world underwater."

I'd asked him what the most beautiful thing he'd ever seen during a dive was.

His face had lit up, and he'd answered me in an instant.

"The shark."

"Weren't you afraid?"

"No, it's beautiful. I had a surge of adrenaline, but a shark is magnificent when it's alive. It moves with a solemn slowness. It's an emperor. Spectacular."

And his whole body was vibrating with joy.

"A Pà, you know that I still see the dead? When the evening news is on and they report on rescues on the open sea, I feel like crying every single time. And if I'm alone at home, I don't know, if my wife and my daughters have gone out, then there it is: The tears stream down my face without asking. They're going to have to take me to see a psychologist, they ought to have forced me to go talk to someone at the time. The dead people that I saw in the hold of that refugee boat? I still have them all right here inside me. But today I went right out and dived at that very same spot. Just like that, on the spur of the moment, without a thought for the conse-quences. And you know something? On the shipwreck lying on the bottom of the sea, there's now coral, there's seaweed, there are fish swimming all around. The first time there was nothing but corpses, but now the sea has transformed everything. I saw an overcoming of death. A return to life, that's what I mean. Sorry, I don't know how to put it any better than that, but I know that you understand me, Pà. I know that you get what I'm trying to say."

Paola took the last two drags on her cigarette and then crushed it out, insisting in the action, repeatedly. The smoke rapidly dissipated.

Paola smiled at Simone and he smiled back.

Suddenly, she got up from the table.

"Melo, come on, open the window, I have to start frying the eggplants for lunch."

Melo's eyes sparkled.

"But can't you open it?"

"No, you do it."

"Why me?"

"You open it better."

And she went over to the stove.

Melo, who hadn't said a word all day, started complaining again.

"It's too hot out, I can't stand to stay up, what kind of pasta are you cooking?"

"Swordfish and eggplant."

"With calamint?"

"Of course."

"All right then, I'll make the effort and stay awake until lunch, but then I'm going to take a nap."

Simone had gone out, informing us that he was going to swing by his house and pick up some wine, and after a shower he'd be back by one, one thirty, two at the very latest.

"Hey, ciao, Beppuzzo."

That evening of October 2, Uncle Beppe still had something to tell me.

He was tired, but he didn't want to hang up.

"Daviduzzo, hold on, there's one last thing I want to tell you, still in reference to the way circles close. It's also about the work you do. In the bed next to mine, there's a young Libyan, he's a minor, he arrived with his father aboard a refugee boat. They landed on Lampedusa. This boy suffers from a very serious form of leukemia. His father watches over him. He's a very dignified person. He often prays next to his son, in a low voice. This gentleman understands Italian and we talked for a while. 'Maybe there's just one God with many different names,' I told him. 'Can you pray a little for me?' And he took my hand in his and started praying in Arabic, and the sounds that he made in that litany were truly so sweet, so different from the shouted prayers that we hear on TV. It touched me. Then he laid his hand on my forehead and blew on it, his fingers opened, and the prayer was over. I immediately thought about the circles that close, Daviduzzo, you're writing about Lampedusa and about me, too, and here I am with two people who landed on Lampedusa of all places, in refugee boats. And, deep in my heart, I blessed our health system, which offers the same care and the same amount of attention to me, who's worked in these structures for years, and to this young man, who faced the open sea, and that's how it ought to be, so he and I are neighbors, in adjoining beds, in this hospital room, fighting together for something as wonderful as life itself."

Then we said goodbye and everything, at that moment, truly seemed to be the next to last chapter of a story coming to an end.

At my grandparents' home, in Uncle Beppe's bedroom, there was a stuffed caiman. Uncle Rocco had brought it back, the same uncle who had given him the frangipani, when he returned from his adventures in Central America. When he came back to Sicily, he'd stepped off the ship with this stuffed caiman under his arm, a gift for his sister, my grandmother. She hadn't liked it a bit, but Uncle Beppe had, my grandfather abstained, and so the decision ultimately fell to my father, who had a tremendous influence over his mother. Papà insisted that he found it to be wonderful, and so that absurd stuffed caiman entered Beppe's bedroom and remained there, atop his clothes closet, like a benevolent guardian. Whenever I spent the night at my grandparents', I always slept in my uncle's bedroom. He hadn't lived in Palermo for years. I would greet the caiman with a respectful nod of the head, then I'd sit down at the large desk, which had a glass surface and drawers on either side. In one drawer was all the foreign coins from the many countries my uncle had visited. In the other, there were many skeletons of fountain pens. I could observe the traces of his life in those objects, fantasizing about where they came from. I looted the clothes closet. It was full of his T-shirts. They fit me perfectly. Over the years, I tried them all on. It was a way of feeling close to him. Those T-shirts had a whiff of America and Northern Europe about them, and I felt handsome when I wore them, less intimidated by girls. In a corner across from the armoire, next to the khaki green sofa bed, there stood a very old classical guitar with metal strings. Uncle, when I was a little boy, and before his fingers forgot the four miserable chords he'd ever learned, used to play "Rock 'n' Roll Suicide" for me, whispering the whole song to me, because he was ashamed—*si affruntàva*—to sing it aloud.

When he had gone to study in America, he'd gone to Coney Island.

"I even swam in the ocean there! It was May, it was so cold."

A plunge into the water off the beach of his heroes.

"And what was the ocean like there?" I asked.

"What do you think it was like? It was a filthy mess."

And he laughed with that wonderful laughter of his that sounded like a little boy who knows he's done something daring, in which innocence and mischief coexist in an inextricable knot, and a tenacious lust for life continued to gleam in the depths of his eyes.

Papà and I went out onto the veranda.

The air was rife with the fleshy aroma of fried eggplant.

"Papà, Beppe was really sick."

"I know. I called him this morning."

The sea was flat as a table. No wind ruffled the waters. It was green, it was azure, it was dark blue.

"What did he say to you?"

"He had some kind of problem with his gallbladder. There might be gallstones in the biliary tract and probably they've shifted. It's the last thing we needed."

My father stared out at the horizon. He kept his arms folded across his chest, to help him think, to ease the burden on his shoulders of his own medical expertise.

"But I talked to him last night. He told me that it was nothing but a fever and that he was getting better. He even told me about the guy in the other bed."

"He was just trying to keep from worrying you."

The sound of the waves on the sand suddenly seemed incredibly loud to me.

"What does he have?"

"Discomfort, pain, nausea. He needs a surgical intervention to remove the gallstones, probably with an endoscopy. The operation in and of itself isn't that serious. But the thing is with his immune system as depressed as it is now, as a direct consequence of the chemo, even the slightest trifle can result in a catastrophic outcome. Beppe asked: 'Couldn't the gallbladder have waited a year, and piped up only once we were through with the tumor?'"

I felt a knot in my stomach.

"How is he?"

"He's depressed. This morning he told me again about the frangipani, about the satisfaction all this late blooming gives him. He identifies with it. It's a thought that in some sense helps him to get through to the end of each day: As long as the plant is thriving, nothing can happen to me."

That morning I'd wondered why my father still hadn't done a photographic portrait of his brother.

And now I'd just understood.

No photograph can be more precise than the feelings you have toward someone you love. They were more than brothers. They were a shared vocabulary, written from the very beginning of their lives.

My breathing had turned irregular.

Would everything be lost, or would it be accepted into something bigger?

"Papà, is Uncle dying?"

I didn't want to make the same mistake I had made with Totò.

I needed to talk about what was hurting me.

My father placed his hand on my shoulder.

I turned to look at him.

In the deeper wrinkles, in the whiteness of his hair, in the marks of time carved into his face, I could read forty-two years of life, my life.

Staring at me with his pale blue eyes, Papà threw his arms wide, both palms turned up to heaven, shrugged his shoulders, and slowly shook his head.

He didn't know.

He couldn't know.

No one can tell the future.

Then, with a nod of his head, he pointed to what lay before us.

The sea lay before us.

It was beautiful, and that beauty was deeply moving.

He was right.

There was nothing else to be done.

Water the frangipani, admire its buds, savor its scent, live in the present, while trying to remain dignified whatever might happen next.

And so I set aside my anxiety and consigned myself to the happy thoughts that made me feel good: the summer my father taught me to swim, my outings with my uncle, Silvia's embrace, the scent of calamint and fried eggplant that had now taken command of the air. And in the meantime my breathing calmed down and Papà and I took off our T-shirts, shoes, and pants, remaining in our swimsuits, and we dove into the water and we were swimming, blessed by the dog-day noon heat, one beside the other, heading for the point of the cove, one stroke after the other, hands spread wide to take it all in, the day sliding away over our flesh, and the horizon before us, firm, unattainable, and boundless.

They weren't gallstones.

It was the lymphoma that was pushing in all directions.

Uncle Beppe's body was breaking apart from inside.

"We're going to have to do a second round of chemo."

Papà's voice over the phone was measured.

"I'm afraid this is the last thing we needed, the very last thing we needed."

It was in the silences between the words that the anguish nestled.

He was spending more time in Reggio than Palermo these days.

It was more likely that you'd find my uncle in the hematology ward than at home.

When I went to visit him in the hospital, what struck me immediately was the thinness of his face. His cheeks were gaunt, his cheekbones projected sharply, the same as Totò's had. It was death that sucks you hollow, drying up the water of life, stripping the flesh from a human being. Inside, even his bones must be trembling. But his eyes. There, now that was it. Uncle's eyes hadn't changed. The gaze was the same: ironic, full of wonder. A good gaze. Child's eyes on loan to an adult body that was falling apart.

"He's really sick," I told Silvia, clutching her tight in an embrace.

His condition was deteriorating daily.

The raft kept taking on water.

My father didn't eat food, he devoured it. He cut his meat with excessive force, fork and knife clattered continuously against the plate. The bites he took were always too large, he chewed vigorously, as if he wanted to bite the whole table. He was sitting down, but his legs never stopped moving.

"I'm going to take a swim," he'd say to my mother at the front door of the house. But it wasn't true. He wasn't going to take a swim in the pool. Papà was going to deliver punches to the water.

Three days before Christmas, there was another complication: The doctors had found fluid in Beppe's peritoneum.

"Is that serious, Papà?"

"Yes."

Papà looked at me the exact same way I must have looked at him years and years ago, when we found ourselves deep in the dense heart of Nature.

"Should we go see Beppe together?"

"Yes, Papà, of course we should."

"Tomorrow?"

"We can leave at six in the morning. I'll drive."

"Thanks."

"You don't need to thank me. I'm glad we're going together to see Uncle Beppe."

During the trip we talked about Avedon's portraits, Capa's photos in Sicily, Koudelka's dogs in the snow. We kept death out of the car.

On the ferry, we went up to the passenger deck.

"Crossing the strait is always so nice."

The wind tousled my hair.

"Yes, it's beautiful."

The whole time, Papà stared at Sicily as we left it behind us.

It was the anticipation of a letting go.

In the last visit that I'd taken to Reggio, I'd brought Uncle a copy of these notes of mine, printed and bound. They stopped on October 3, with me and Papà swimming at Cala Pisana.

"Here you are, Beppuzzo, I hurried up, I wrote it."

"What's it called?"

"*Notes on a Shipwreck.*"

"So is it true that I'm in it, too?"

"Yes."

"And my brother, too?"

"Yes."

"Can I read it?"

"That's why I brought it."

He started it immediately, despite the fact that he was tired because the night before he'd been unable to sleep. It took him two days. Even just turning the page cost him effort. When he was done, he asked me: "There's one thing I don't understand. There are so many shipwrecks in here. What about me? Do I have a landing?"

The whole time he held my hand in his, caressing my hand with his slender fingers. I sat there in silence, without answering, just looking at him and nothing else. I still hadn't understood that the answer was all there, in the caressing of our hands.

In the hospital, we ran into Silvana.

"Beppe has just been taken to the operating room."

The fluid they had found in his peritoneum was due to the lymphoma.

There were enlarged lymph nodes everywhere.

They'd even started to compress his kidney.

"They're inserting a stent into his urethra."

The only chance was to start a third round of chemo.

"The chemo of desperation," said Papà.

Uttering those words must have cost him a tremendous stab of pain.

"Beppe is lucid, in any case. The final decision will be up to him."

Uncle's ankles were swollen, his legs were swollen, his belly was swollen, his stomach was swollen, his face was gaunt. I saw him on the gurney, as he emerged from the operating room. They were taking him back to the hematology ward.

"We'll see you in the afternoon," I said to him.

Uncle saw me, understood what I'd said, and smiled at me.

He'd wait for me.

We'd still have a moment all for us.

———————

My first memory of Beppe dates back to when I was two years old. Mamma and Papà had left me alone with him for a couple of hours, during which time Uncle had taken me around with him through the underbelly of Palermo. Until then, my parents had fed me only select and delicate foods. Uncle Beppe let me eat *pane e panelle*, bread and chickpea fritters. Two hours with him eradicated any and all control they had over my diet. Mamma and Papà were so stunned at his response—"Oh well, how could *pane e panelle* ever do him any harm?"—that they decided to take it as the pure gospel truth.

From that day forward, I started eating more or less everything and anything. Even now, I have a cast iron stomach. I'm firmly convinced that it was a result of that baptism with street food, in which my uncle served as my godfather.

In the end, it's simple: for me, Uncle Beppe is the taste of bread and chickpea fritters.

At four o'clock, the first to return to the ward was Papà. He was wearing his lab coat and his shoe covers, and he went straight to his brother. Beppe asked for him continuously, especially at night, when his fever and the darkness led him to seek protection. The two brothers stayed close, they observed each other, and their two worlds fit together to perfection.

When Papà left the ward, it was my turn to wrap the green hospital gown around me and tie it in the back.

"He's expecting you, he's lucid."

It was if he'd been gentled by that last encounter, and the fact that he knew that I was going to be seeing his brother seemed to me to be a cause of some further serenity in him.

When I stepped close to the bed, Uncle Beppe recognized me immediately.

"Daviduzzo."

His voice was a whisper.

He took my hand in his and did something that I truly wasn't expecting.

He started to sob.

"No, Beppuzzo, don't cry."

He stopped immediately. The tears trembled on the rims of his eyes and he was holding his breath. And yet, even at that moment, his extraordinary ability to listen glittered once again, suspending the impetus of his tears, damming back his fear. My uncle was sincerely curious to listen to me.

And I, I had eyes of calmness, I breathed calmly, my heart beat calmly in my rib cage.

"If you were alone in a hospital bed, Uncle, with no one who ever came to see you, then you'd have every right to cry. But have you seen how many people come to see you? In the waiting room, I've met your colleagues and your patients who've all come to see you, your nurses and your students. And lots and lots of friends are asking about you, at home and on the phone. Those are genuine relationships, Uncle. Human relations transcend time."

Beppe started to nod.

"And after all we're the two of us, Beppuzzo. You and me. We have a beautiful relationship, it's been going on since I was born and it'll last the rest of my life. Because the scale of our history tends toward goodness, doesn't it, Uncle?"

He nodded, his big eyes watching me. Inside them, there quivered a boundless love. There weren't eyes on earth deep enough to hold that love.

"For me, you'll never be a memory, Uncle. You'll never be a recollection. Time happens in the present. And in my present our relationship exists always. You're always with me. In the constellation of my existence, you're one of the brightest stars. And this is what stars do: They transcend time to show us the way."

He caressed the back of my hand with his thumb, brushing my palm with his fingertips.

What gentle hands you've always had, Uncle.

"Daviduzzo, I'd like to live a few more years."

"We'd all like that, all of us. But one or two or ten more years wouldn't change a jot or a tittle of what we've built together."

Uncle gave a faint smile.

"So don't cry," he whispered.

"There's too much beauty to cry," I replied.

And he let his childish smile bloom into his face. I gave him a kiss on the forehead and left.

"How did he strike you?" Papà asked me. He was vibrating.

"We talked. We made peace with each other."

I told him about that conversation of ours and I could see his tension lessen, the lines of his face relax, his breathing become more regular. Papà's foot had stopped and his gaze had come to rest on me. "It's incredible how people go through phases," he mused.

"First there's the disbelief, 'It can't be happening to me,' then comes denial, 'They must have made a mistake, there's no tumor,' then comes anger, and then comes depression, 'But why me of all people?' and then a sort of peace, and last of all, what I experienced myself when I was in there, the phase in which it's Beppe who consoles those of us who remain behind. As if, with the approach of death, they were able to perceive something that isn't given to us to see in life, and which makes those who are about to die merciful toward those who remain on this side of life."

Papà put his lab coat on and went back to the ward to visit his brother.

Now the way he walked was different.

He wasn't walking like a doctor anymore.

Now he was walking like an elder brother.

The third chemo never began, it would just have been therapeutic savagery. Beppe was released from the hospital and sent home. Colleagues came to see him from all over Italy, physicians he'd trained, friends, relatives. Every single time, my uncle asked to be aided to sit in his chair, so that he could receive each visitor sitting upright.

I had one regret, that I hadn't swum with my uncle in the sea off the island.

I read Uncle this note that I'd jotted down.

Lampedusa, from *lepas*, the shoals that take the skin off you, eroded by the fury of the elements, that resist and confirm a presence, however solitary, in the boundless vastness of the open sea. Or else, Lampedusa from *lampas*, the torch that gleams in the darkness, light that defeats the darkness.

"What do you say, should I add it to the novel, Uncle?"

"Yes, put it at the end, it's nice to end with light and with resistance."

He died in his bed in late December.

He'd asked everyone not to cry.

"Only now that he's dead do I realize what beautiful hands my brother had," Papà confessed to me.

The first night without uncle went by quietly.

The sun still hadn't risen when I walked out onto the balcony.

Sicily in front of me had just emerged from the contemplation of the night, as it had the day before, and the day before that, all the way back to the end of days.

You could perceive the dawn.

It was still hesitating, held back by the sea.

I leaned against the railing and waited for its rays on my body.